Civil Architecture

The New Public Infrastructure

Civil Architecture

The New Public Infrastructure

Richard Dattner, *FAIA*

Library of Congress Cataloging-in-Publication Data

Dattner, Richard.
    Civil architecture : the new public infrastructure / Richard
Dattner.
       p.   cm.
    Includes bibliographical references and index.
    ISBN 0-07-015665-4
    1. Public architecture.   I. Title.
   NA9050.5.D38   1994
   725—dc20   94-41778
                                                 CIP

1 2 3 4 5 6 7 8 9 0 KP/KP 9 0 9 8 7 6 5 4

ISBN 0-07-015665-4

*The sponsoring editor for this book was Joel Stein. This book was
set in Janson and Gill Sans by North Market Street Graphics.*

Printed and bound by Kingsport Press.

Civil Architecture is dedicated to the many individuals whose contributions were essential for the realization of the work illustrated:

Joseph Coppola, William Stein, Bernard Zipprich, Beth Greenberg and Frances Soliven—valued associates, colleagues and friends.

The architects, architects-in-training and administrators who have shared in these efforts and made their special contributions.

The client organizations, agencies and public servants commissioning and overseeing these projects.

And all those whose previous labors have created the civil environment in which our present efforts take place.

Contents

Jefferson's "Lawn"
University of Virginia

"Architecture is my delight . . . it is an enthusiasm of which I am not ashamed, as its object is to improve the taste of my countrymen, to increase their reputation, to reconcile them to the rest of the world, and procure them its praise."

Thomas Jefferson, 1791

"Think Globally, Act Locally"

Bumper Sticker, 1994

Introduction

This book is about the architecture we build for our communal, public, civic life. Titling it *Public Architecture* was an option which, although close in meaning, would have missed some of the grander connotations of "civil." *Civic Architecture* was closer to my intended theme but also missed certain meanings resonating around "civil"—civility, civilization, civil engineering.

It also skirted presumptuously close to the title of *Civic Art*—the monumental and encyclopedic compendium of city planning, design of plazas, gardens and streets, and examples of campus planning published by Warner Hegemann and Elbert Peets in 1922 under the full title of *The American Vitruvius: An Architect's Handbook of Civic Art*. The 70 years since that work have not diminished its central theme: the importance of design in the built environment we share as a society. What has changed, to a degree difficult to imagine in 1922, is the nature between private and public life, the relationship of that public life and the buildings built to accommodate it.

Private and Public

Public life is endangered and we retreat from it into a condition of "privateness" ("privacy" should be the appropriate word, but we are also in trouble there). Public figures are suspect, public spaces seen as potentially dangerous, public facilities perceived as sub-standard. Where once public activity was considered a pleasant, entertaining, uplifting experience, now it is increasingly avoided. Saturday nights at the movies and Sundays in the local park have been replaced for many by a rented video and hours in the car. Sitting around the electronic campfire, or in our private cars, we encapsulate ourselves.

Our interests are increasingly private ones. Contemporary magazines and books show us how to improve our bodies, wardrobes, homes. Television parades individuals baring their most private thoughts and experiences to millions of strangers. Having successfully retreated into our private zone we spend our time looking at the ostensibly private lives of others for diversion. Something is wrong here, too.

Private life derives part of its value from the tension between its familiarity, intimacy, and individual concerns and the attributes of public life—civility, community, ceremony, spectacle, responsibility for others. The diminishment of the public sphere disturbs the balance needed for a healthy, civilized existence and by this imbalance diminishes our private world. The alarming rise of homelessness of families and individuals is paralleled by a public homelessness. To the extent that public parks become defacto homeless shelters, they cease being public.

We inhabit both a private and a public world. Just as our homes express our individual situation and personal values, so does our public, built environment express our communal, social values. We furnish our private homes with furniture, appliances, carpeting, art. We furnish our public world with city halls, courthouses, schools, plazas, parks and playgrounds, post offices, bridges, sewage treatment plants, police stations, jails. This book is about our shared, public, civic home.

Public and Civil

Public is a resonant word in a democratic society: public school, public park, public works. Derived from the Latin *populus*—the people—it defines several of the necessary attributes of Civil Architecture:

- belonging to the community as a whole
- open to common use

The Latin *civis*—citizen—defined a person having the additional rights and responsibilities of citizenship. Civic participation—voting, deliberation of public issues, owning property—was restricted to citizens. The *populus*—populace—were the masses, the mob.

In our society, this ancient distinction has lost much of its former meaning, but echoes remain. Recent increases in illegal immigration have created a class of millions of people without access to the full rights of citizenship or responsibility for supporting these privileges. Significant segments of our population avoid taxation in underground economies, avoid participation in public issues, avoid the vote. They are members of the public, but are not citizens in the full meaning of the word.

Civil differs from public primarily in its connotations of responsibility to others, to society, to one's surroundings. Among its meanings are:

- of citizens
- of a community of citizens, their government, their interrelations
- civilized, brought out of a condition of barbarism, instructed in the ways of an advanced society
- suitable for a city dweller, not rustic or countrified
- urbane, polite, respectful of the rights of others
- not military or ecclesiastical
- civil architecture; the architecture which is employed in constructing buildings for the purposes of civil life

Architect and Citizen

This book is written out of a conviction that an appropriate, noble, dignified, accessible civil architecture is absolutely essential to our individual
well-being as citizens, and to our collective well-being as a society: appropriate in its respect of user and context; noble in expressing the importance
of civic life; dignified in its avoidance of fads; accessible and inviting to
users, staff, and passers-by. We make our civil architecture, and it renders
our shared values in concrete, stone, metal and glass. For a long time after
its completion, this built heritage "makes" us, especially when we are
young, by transmitting the values of the generation which built it. The
schoolhouse teaches its own lessons—speaks—to children who listen.

Public Childhood

My concern with the civility, order and accessibility of a shared public
environment had its genesis in the incivility, chaos and terror of the
wartime Poland my parents and I fled in 1940. As a young immigrant first
to Italy, then to Cuba, and finally to the United States before reaching my
ninth birthday, I was especially sensitive to each of these new cultures.
And, as each new language was superimposed on those preceding, the non-
verbal syntax of form, light and place became for me the constant language
with which I am still most at home.

Several, mostly public schools are etched into my memory, each with a
"voice" distinct and unforgettable. The first, in 1941 when I was four, was
a nursery group in an internment camp in the south of Italy. I was with my
mother, my father having been temporarily removed to an adjoining camp
for men. My parents later described the warmth of our Italian hosts, and
showed me photos of the camp and my first school. The following scene is
my only memory of both camp and school: a gate through a barbed wire
fence, a group of children and a teacher, a young woman, are passing
through this gate. Behind us is the camp of wooden barracks, clotheslines,
heat; ahead of us a meadow of tall grass and flowers reaching to the brow
of a hill which seemed to touch a sky with cotton clouds. In the midst of
a situation with a potential (I now know) for the most terrible consequences, my school was an open gate, a green meadow, the sky, a temporary freedom.

My second school (in order only, numbered schools were still to come)
was a two-story stucco villa of tall rooms with large, shuttered windows in
World War II Havana. Saint George's was a school for the upper, educated
class. The teachers were Cuban, American and English, the yearbook of

0.1. Postcard view of Delaware Park in Buffalo. Designed by Frederick Law Olmsted, it formed the setting for the Pan-American Exposition of 1901.

the graduating class of 1946 was almost entirely in English. Not strictly a public school, it functioned as such—the school of choice—for those of us in the large refugee community. The school was a wonderful mix of European order, discipline and reverence for learning softened by the warmth of the Caribbean and the Cuban temperament. It was an island of temporary privilege and good fortune in a sea of poverty in which, outside the restaurants, the homeless begged for food. A fenced, paved courtyard served as a playground; the formal entrance was on the opposite side of the school, through a wrought iron gate, up a stair and across a portico. The fence and gate were there mostly to keep out those who did not belong and the windows of all the buildings were barred.

In the fall of 1946, school was P.S. 152 in Jackson Heights, Queens, New York City. My memories now become increasingly populated by schoolmates, but recollections of the rooms, hallways, and stairs remain as the backgrounds of these vignettes. The four- or five-story school (I never reached those upper worlds) was impressive, antiseptic, somewhat unfriendly. Perhaps the contrast with my former school intensified the apparent noise and harshness of this building. Cuban floors had been hard and cool, these were hard and noisy. I mostly remember P.S.152 through a scrim of wire mesh—chain link in the asphalt, tree-less playground, woven wire in the narrow stairs like cattle pens, with different pens for going up or down.

The winter of 1946 (three schools in two countries in one year!) brought me to P.S. 16 in Buffalo, New York. I know it now as a gargantuan version of a one-room schoolhouse, a narrow, four-story Victorian pile of dark brick organized around a single front-to-back corridor on each floor. The height we kids could reach was memorialized, like a high water mark, by a dark oak wainscot in the hallways, near the top of which floated illuminated milk glass globes suspended on long chains.

We sat at gouged wooden desks whose tops opened to reveal storage for our books, pens, pencils. The front, immovable part of the desktop had a hole housing a glass jar which was daily filled with ink by one of us so graced with this responsibility. The desks, chairs (attached), teacher's desk and shelves were, or seemed, immovable. If we could be maintained in a similar state of immobility while our teachers taught us, we would be educated. Adjoining each classroom and serving as a kind of entrance foyer was a cloakroom. Here, out of sight of the teacher, and therefore mobile, we could fool around while putting on the coats, scarves, mittens, and galoshes which would protect us from a Tolstoyan death by freezing.

When spring came, the arching elms whose branches met a hundred feet above most streets burst into leaf, and, by summer, a virtually unbro-

0.2. Lafayette High School: Architects Esenwein and Johnson designed this imposing structure in 1903 to tower above its Buffalo neighborhood of modest frame houses. *Photo: Buffalo Erie County Historical Society.*

ken canopy shaded the sidewalks far below. The widest streets had four tree-rows which, across the wide streets and narrow sidewalks, created a cathedral of shimmering nave and aisles. It was a vision of civic grandeur. Long, wide public streets of trees sheltered endless rows of private homes, each one the duplicate of, and just slightly different from, its neighbor.

At the end of fifth grade we moved and I completed sixth through eighth grades at P.S. 52, in another Buffalo neighborhood. This was, at that time, a "new" school, having been built during the Works Progress Administration, that unsurpassed period of public construction during the Great Depression. Its architectural expression was simple and direct. If it did not try to uplift the spirits of its users, neither did it offend. Much like Buffalo itself, it was designed to do the job required of it. In my memory, the classrooms seem unable to contain the multiple explosions taking place within them: raging hormones, changing voices (mostly boys), changing figures (mostly girls). Only the bigger spaces—auditorium, gymnasium, and playground—had a scale which seemed commensurate to our expanding needs and capabilities.

Public High School

While primary schools around the world seem to share many qualities, the American public high school is, in my mind, uniquely ours. A microcosm of our society, it is in varying part school, corporation, theater, sports club, factory, army, church, jail. I attended two such institutions.

Lafayette High School was a remnant of that civic golden age when Buffalo was still the second largest rail freight center in the country, and was about to become a mighty industrial city whose grain towers, steel mills and blast furnaces would stretch for miles along the Lake Erie shore. Rising five stories above a neighborhood of wood frame houses with its towers and mansard roofs, it had been since 1903 a cathedral of learning and neighborhood landmark. Only the stately elms reached up as high, but they were, already in this year of 1951, dying of Dutch Elm disease.

Inside the school, next to the obligatory Winslow Homer scenes, framed mottoes urged us to embrace the values of the hard-working immigrants from Germany, Italy, Ireland, and Poland whose energy and money had built Buffalo and that school: "What You Are To Be, You Are Now Becoming," "Be Strong, And Of A Good Courage." The principal, appropriately named Mr. Gott, was a nineteenth-century figure, in buttoned suit and starched collar, who ruled the premises in a formal, distant manner. The boys' subterranean locker rooms were ruled by gangs which periodically pushed the lockers over like dominoes, splattered oranges and other

0.3. Bennett High School, Buffalo: A modest, boxy building rendered monumental by a columned and pedimented entrance facade and broad, terraced steps.

edibles against the walls, and generally oppressed those of us whose predilections were more intellectual. As I said, a microcosm of our society.

Bennett High School was my refuge for junior and senior years, it was the school whose common expectation was that we were college-bound, were headed "out of town." The building was, in floor plan, identical to most of the other Buffalo high schools (and many others throughout the state) but its exterior treatment introduced variation into the prototype. A Georgian, columned and pedimented entrance at the culmination of broad, terraced steps climbing from Main Street, created a certain civic monumentality and importance to what would have otherwise been a plain and homely building. The undecorated, unseen (from Main Street) rear facade looked out over a football field and stadium of significant size. (High school football mattered in Buffalo. On a bitter winter night in 1954, 55,000 freezing spectators watched Bennett play its archrival, Kensington High School, for the championship. I don't remember who won, but the intensity and passion of players and spectators at that game overshadow, for me, any public event seen since.)

A city in miniature, Bennett functioned to assimilate us into the adult world which waited, like the pharmacists, accountants and businessmen hosting our attendance at Kiwanis Key Club luncheons, for our expected, willing collaboration. The few African-American students were either part of our college-bound crowd, or good at basketball and loudly cheered at games. Few such cross-cultural friendships survived the 4 P.M. dispersal home.

There were serpents in this Western New York Garden of Eden— fights (with fists, mostly), occasional muggings, drunkenness, family abuse. The largely immigrant Polish, Italian and German population was about to be squeezed between the departure of the steel mills and other industrial plants which had supported them and the arrival of large numbers of poor, southern blacks seeking precisely that employment when it was already disappearing. Verlyn Klinkenborg's prose poem, *The Last Fine Time*, captures brilliantly this Buffalo moment. A companion book, *Coming Of Age In Buffalo*, by William Graebner, offers a scholarly look at teenagers in those years of 1952–57, a sort of golden age of American teen culture.

I dwell on these public schools because, as children, we spent so much time in them, and because of their importance in helping to create the next generation of *citizens*. (Prisons and shelters have an equivalent impact, but their clients are by the time they reach them so overwhelmed by their problems, that education for citizenship is an option for very few.)

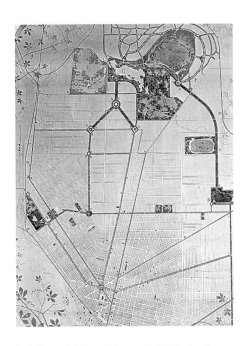

0.4. Frederick Law Olmsted's 1874 plan for Buffalo's park system. Like Haussman's contemporaneous boulevards in Paris, wide, landscaped parkways were superimposed on the former street grid. *Courtesy of National Park Service Frederick Law Olmsted Natural Historic Site.*

Woven into this constant fabric of public schools were the occasional strands of other public buildings and places: the one-room public library where you could borrow (for free!) six books at a time; the elephantine, phallic, Art Deco City Hall where one went for birth certificates and learner's permits; the beautiful, Gothic main public library shortly to be demolished and replaced by a more efficient structure of immeasurable banality; the city jail we visited as an object lesson of the price exacted for civil disobedience.

And, finally, like a necklace of vast value, largely ignored, a skein of public parks and boulevards laid out by Frederick Law Olmsted in the late 1860's, bejeweled by classic remnants of the Pan-American Exposition of 1901. Like Chicago's Columbian Exposition of 1893, this international fair intended to elevate its host city to international status. Mostly remembered now as the site of President McKinley's assassination, it nonetheless gave Buffalo an armature of civic grandeur, order and beauty which lasted almost 60 years, until post-war suburbanization, industrial obsolescence, Dutch Elm disease, and racial discord erased so much of it.

In retrospect, I am filled with wonder and appreciation at what could be accomplished in that world of civic riches by a nine-year-old immigrant using public schools and libraries, riding public trolleys and busses, playing in public parks and streets. This miracle continues every day as new immigrants—future citizens—learn their way into our shared society and add something of their native heritage to it.

Citizen and Civil Architect

After high school, life seems to speed up. I left Buffalo for the Massachusetts Institute of Technology, and rediscovered a passion for architecture dormant since primary school. MIT's architecture program was wonderfully diverse, with design approaches as varied as the faculty of practicing architects. Two lecturers nearing the end of their professional careers particularly influenced my consciousness.

Lewis Mumford illuminated the link between architecture and the culture in which it is created. Tracing urban settlements to their earliest examples, he demonstrated that urban form was the manifestation of political structure and systems of belief. He was an early "de-constructor" of the built environment, combining a wide-ranging intelligence with the now increasingly rare ability of communicating intelligibly. Joseph Hudnut's illustrated lectures on architectural history taught, as a sub-text, the primacy of substance over style. His long career had spanned a number of

0.5. The Casino and Lake in Olmsted and Vaux's Delaware Park on a summer day in 1900. White shirts, dark skirts, a picture of civic order. In the following year, a few blocks from here, President McKinley would be assassinated. *Photo: Buffalo Erie County Historical Society.*

stylistic periods (he had been instrumental in bringing Gropius to Harvard) and his wry humor and sense of irony lent an almost biblical detachment to his opinions about contemporary architecture.

The third year of my five-year program was at the Architectural Association in London. In that year of 1957, London was undergoing a massive reconstruction of the public infrastructure destroyed during the war. The London County Council, with a large team of municipal planners and architects (something like New York during the WPA), was designing and building hundreds of new public schools and thousands of new public housing units.

To be a student of architecture in that time and place was to share the conviction that architecture and planning could make a difference in people's lives. My teachers at the Architectural Association—the British "New Brutalists" James Stirling, James Gowan, Peter and Alison Smithson—were looking for a direction for modern architecture which would express the striving for social justice, the limited resources available, and the growing complexity of post-war urban life. In the shared poverty following the destruction of the war, the public sector took on an increased importance.

I graduated from M.I.T., served in the Army at Fort Dix, New Jersey, settled in New York, started an architectural practice, and found myself increasingly involved with the design of buildings and spaces for public use: *Civil Architecture*. The intervening years have been marked by a dangerous regression in the quality of public life which threatens our civility and our civilization. The homeless and disoriented people begging in the streets of our cities are worse off and more threatening than the beggars in Havana. The destruction of entire urban neighborhoods is worse than that of London in that it came from within, and there is less hope for its reversal.

Architecture for public use is both constant and changing. The constants include the need to educate, transmit social values, shelter, provide clean water, carry away sewage and garbage, protect from dangerous behavior. The means of providing these civic facilities and their built form undergo significant changes which mirror the changes in society itself. Consider these recent projects from the author's architectural practice:

- A public school where the architect was selected by a committee of teachers, parents and local community representatives, rather than by the Board of Education. This group continued to meet regularly with the architectural team for the duration of the design process, having a say in almost every aspect of the realized project.

- A public park built on the 28-acre roof enclosing a sewage treatment plant, in a 15-year process of accommodating a community opposed to the construction of the plant in their neighborhood. The sewage plant was built despite their protest, but the park reflected an ultimately successful collaboration between the community, the design team and Federal, State, and City governments.

- A new public school built in a former corporate headquarters building donated to the Board of Education, operated and funded by a private foundation.

- A world-class competition swimming facility built by a non-profit organization with private donations on public land, which also includes a sports medicine facility operated by a major medical center.

- A marine transfer station for dumping trucked garbage into barges whose entrance replicates the Victorian facade of the replaced original building which, in turn, replicated an ancient Roman prototype.

- A rehabilitation park containing a replica of the outside world in a manageable and forgiving form.

- Collaboration with noted artists on public art planned as an integral feature of public buildings.

Civil Architecture

The realization of civil architecture requires civility, compromise, improvisation, accommodation, patience, tenacity and a sense of humor. The need for public structures grows as public resources diminish and bureaucracies expand. If architects were likened to doctors, architects designing public facilities would be closest to physicians attending emergency rooms—practicing in public view, balancing conflicting requirements first, focusing on essentials, constantly evaluating priorities. The injunction "to do no harm" applies to both professions equally, as does the immense responsibility involved, and the satisfaction derived from a successful result.

Architects use their human talents and energy to organize the efforts of others—the skilled tradesmen and women who actually construct buildings—in creating some order from the chaos that will ultimately prevail. (See the digression on the Second Law of Thermodynamics on page 129.)

Introduction

Those who design civil architecture labor at the intersection of their culture's aspirations, political struggles and available resources. It is an exciting place to work.

This book is an account of such a practice, illustrated by projects realized over a period of 30 years, supplemented by a portfolio of significant public architecture by other architects sharing a vision of the importance of such work, and annotated by some personal digressions.

Fire! Fire!

Municipalities have fire departments which can be mobilized in minutes to fight a fire before it goes out of control. Speed up a film of water damage, freezing mortar joints and rusting metal, and it is just as destructive as fire. (Rusting is oxidation, a slow fire. Fire can be thought of as very fast oxidation.) Perhaps municipalities should have a Leak Brigade, *which would be mobilized within 24 hours of the report of* **Leak! Leak!** *in a public structure. Dressed in easily recognizable uniforms (to demonstrate to taxpayers that something is actually being done), they would proceed, calmly and without sirens, to the endangered structure, where they would put out the leak and immediately halt the spread of water. (Fire men and women don't issue reports and findings that buildings are hot and endangered. They put out fires, and they don't leave until there is no further danger of the fire spreading.)*

This is an idea of such simplicity that it is a wonder it has not, to my knowledge, ever been tried. In New York, a close counterpart—a Fire Brigade, privately funded by major fire insurers—answers fire alarms involving department stores and other premises where valuable contents are stored. They are so efficient that they often get to the site of a fire before the Fire Department. Their job (like the Leak Brigade) is to protect both premises and contents from water damage—in this case, the water from the fire fighters.

A follow-up team of architects and engineers (private consultants, hired under annual term contracts balancing cost and demonstrated competence) would prescribe permanent roofing repairs. Such repairs would have to be done within a specified time period; 90 days seems reasonable. The cost of the Leak Brigade and the required permanent roofing repairs would result in ultimate savings of such magnitude that a number of financing techniques could be utilized. It is not unreasonable to expect that every dollar spent in such structural first aid could save between ten and a hundred times its cost in preventing future damage.

Public Recreation

1.1. Croton Park Pool, Bronx, New York. One of the heroic public works of the Robert Moses era. *John MacGilchrist, renderer, New York City Parks Photo Archive.*

The Golden Age of Public Architecture

In the summer of 1936, New York City Parks Commissioner Robert Moses and his group of over a thousand architects, landscape architects and engineers opened 10 outdoor public pools of superlative design. These facilities were so well designed and constructed that they have lasted until now, despite neglect and shoddy maintenance. They represent an urban legacy from the era of the Works Progress Administration (WPA) which is only now being properly recognized and restored. (See the Thomas Jefferson Swim Center and the McCarren Pool Complex discussed elsewhere in this section.) WPA projects in the period 1933-1939 provided American communities with parks, schools, court houses, post offices, government buildings, highways and bridges, as well as less visible improvements to the water supply and sewage systems.

The WPA provided jobs for thousands of architects and engineers who designed projects which would employ hundreds of thousands of construction workers, foresters, and artists. Begun by the Roosevelt Administration to lift the country out of the Great Depression, this vast program of public construction changed our cities, towns and countryside to an unprecedented degree. Only the national mobilization undertaken to wage the Second World War would exceed the scale of the WPA legacy.

1.2. The Astoria Pool complex in Queens, located next to the massive Hell Gate Bridge, was among the grandest of the dozen large public pools completed by Moses in the 1930's. *Photo: Max Ulrich, New York City Parks Photo Archive.*

If the post-depression era was the Golden Age of public construction in America, Robert Moses (NYC Parks Commissioner from 1934 to 1960) was its King Midas, becoming both the most powerful and visionary public builder in the land, and, ultimately, a man perceived as a destroyer of communities and enemy of democracy. (The monumental Robert Caro biography of Moses, *The Power Broker*, is essential for an understanding of this giant and his time.) Moses' early triumphs included bridges, highways, public ocean beaches and the public parkways to bring a newly mobile population to them. His later defeats included attempts to bisect Manhattan by highways at 30th Street and Broome Streets, as well as abortive attempts to bridge the Long Island Sound. His last large victory, the Cross Bronx Expressway, was seen by most planners as a terminal defeat for the communities bisected and ultimately destroyed by its construction.

In the New York City Parks system, the Moses legacy was more benign; the 33 outdoor and seven indoor pools currently in use were largely built or rehabilitated under his tenure. With the 24 more recent "mini" pools built about 20 years ago, over a million swimmers are served each year. But public swimming facilities, along with the rest of the public recreation system, are bearing the brunt of cutbacks in public spending. As the costs of providing public services perceived as more vital—police, fire, sanitation, schools, transportation—continue to rise in a time of economic contraction or stagnation, recreation services and maintenance are often the easiest targets for reducing public spending.

1.3. New York City's Orchard Beach, on the shore of Long Island Sound, was designed in 1936 by Parks Department architect Aymar Embury to be both welcoming and monumental. *New York City Parks Photo Archive.*

Fire and Water

1.4. Karl Marx Hof in Greenpoint, Brooklyn. Heroic civic architecture crumbling because of neglect and political dissention.

1.5. The heroic McCarren Pool entry arch has become a pathetic ruin through neglect and the ravages of the freeze-thaw cycle.

One of the four WPA pools built in Brooklyn, McCarren Pool was designed by the New York City Parks Department with Aymar Embury II, consultant, and completed in 1936. Its vast scale (the main pool measured 165 by 330 feet) recalled the Roman Baths at Caracalla, while the arched central entrance reminded some of the Karl Marx Hof, a sprawling public housing complex built in Vienna in 1929. It embodied the heroic quality which characterized so much of the public construction of that time.

Use It Or Lose It

In appearance and construction a structure that would endure for generations, McCarren Pool was weakened by roof leaks, deferred (read nonexistent) maintenance, and the eventual rusting of the steel reinforcing. The facility was closed in 1981, and the abandoned structure was gutted by fire in 1987. While most of the other large WPA pools were rehabilitated, plans to repair this pool have been stymied by community concerns that such a large facility would attract an uncontrollable number of largely teenage (and ethnically different) users. In the intervening years deterioration has continued to the point that any use of this facility would involve almost total reconstruction.

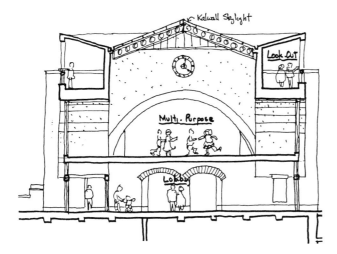

1.6. Enclosing the formerly open arch and adding a new upper level would preserve the entrance while adding a grand multi-purpose room.

1.7. This view from the early years of McCarren Pool suggests what the restored park could look like—a structure of striking modernity and power. *New York City Parks Photo Archive.*

The lesson is a familiar one, although usually ignored: the construction of a public facility must include a commitment to maintain it in perpetuity. Roof leaks can be easily and inexpensively repaired. If they are ignored, the resulting water penetration can cause rapidly escalating damage which can ultimately require massive reconstruction, at a cost often greater than the original cost of the entire original construction.

A New Life for McCarren Pool

While too late to reverse the ravages of time, there is a possible future for this facility which saves what it can from the past and responds to the new social realities and funding constraints. Through an architectural triage, parts of this facility need to be demolished so that the more appropriately scaled remainder can prosper. Design goals would include making this a year-round recreation facility to better justify public expenditure, as well as the preservation of the most unique architectural feature—the grandly arched entrance and clerestory gallery.

The formerly open entry arch would be enclosed with a translucent skylight and window walls, and a new upper level would be inserted within the arches. The enclosed lower level would be the entrance to the rehabilitated complex, with an information/security station, circulation and exhibit space, and elevator and stair access to the new upper level.

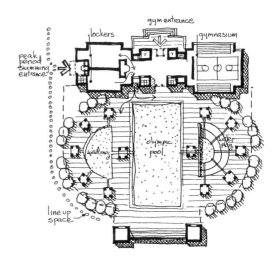

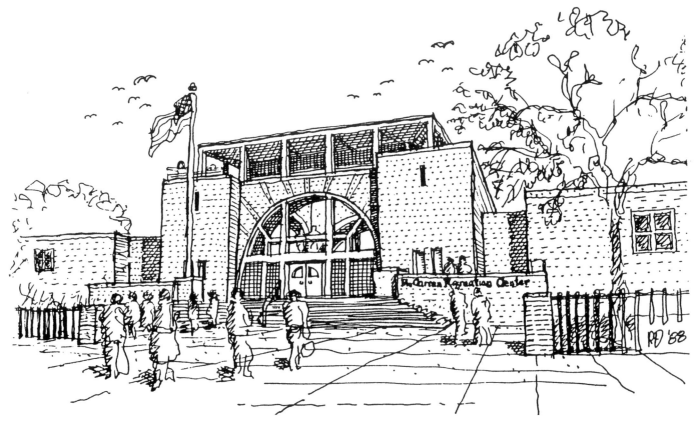

1.8. Enclosure of the entrance arch transforms the pool complex into a year-round recreation facility.

The heavily damaged side wings would be demolished and replaced by smaller, two-story structures of matching brick. One wing would contain locker rooms on the lower level, and smaller spaces on the upper floor. In the summer, pool users would enter these lockers directly from the out-doors and proceed to the outdoor pool, without entering the arched entrance. This would simplify circulation and help control those waiting to enter the pool. The other wing would house a gymnasium with upper-level seating galleries.

The upper level within the arches would be a multi-purpose activity space leading to activity rooms over the locker rooms on one side, and upper-level seating for the gymnasium on the other. The former clerestory would be turned into an observation gallery from which the entire park would be visible.

The outdoor pool would be reduced in size to 50 meters by 25 meters, with a new stainless steel pool wall and gutter system.

1.9. The main pool is reduced in size to facilitate supervision, and the former diving pool is replaced by a wading pool. Peak period pool users bypass the central, year-round entrance.

1.10. The wading pool is fed by water channels from fountains under a series of trellised shade structures.

Wading Pool / Water channel — RO '88

Water Play Area

1.11. Young children play in this terraced water play area fed by channeled waterfalls. In cooler months, this area will find use as an amphitheater.

Guard Platform   RO '88

1.12. Guard platforms respect the original architecture while providing enhanced visibility and control of the swimming pool.

1.13. New AquaCenter in New York City relates architecturally to the parabolic former Municipal Asphalt Plant. *Photo © Michael Ritter.*

A Private/Public Partnership

Although in recent years several of the large outdoor pools had been rehabilitated, no new municipal swimming facilities had been built in New York City for many years, with the notable exception of Riverbank State Park, a state facility more fully described in a separate chapter. The city has a large population needing swimming pools, as most city neighborhoods are lacking in this regard and few schools have pools. It also has a large acreage of mapped park land, much of it in small, hard-to-use parcels, and all of it mandated to be used solely for recreation. What it did not have was the capital construction funding to build a new pool, or funds for operating such a facility. The public sector needed a partner.

The Municipal Asphalt Plant

One of the shining examples of New York City's heritage of public structures is the parabolic Municipal Asphalt Plant designed by Kahn and Jacobs in 1942, and chosen by the then fledgling Museum of Modern Art as one of the ten best designed structures in the U.S. from 1932-1944. In 1968 the production of asphalt for filling New York's legendary potholes was moved elsewhere, the surrounding ancillary structures were torn down, and an unsuccessful attempt was made to demolish the concrete parabola. It would not yield to the wrecker's iron ball and was left in place. As part of urban renewal, the site was designated in 1970 for subsidized housing and a public school, a proposal which met with significant opposition from the neighborhood. Dr. George Murphy and 19 other local residents formed a committee to stop the renewal project and study the potential of preserving the parabola and the surrounding 5-acre site as a recreation center.

From 1972 to 1986 the group lobbied, raised funds, had the parabola declared a landmark, and won permission to recycle the landmark into a mixed-use community center. The concept of a private, non-profit group building and operating a recreation facility under contract with the municipality, on public land, was established and proved successful. Funding for the center (now called Asphalt Green) came from private donations, user fees from local private schools, day-camp fees and other fund-raising sources. The private funding covered operating expenses, and allowed free use of the facility by local public schools and individuals who could not afford to pay. Dr. Murphy and the group he formed had created a local institution which would continue as a self-supporting, community resource. In 1985, another neighborhood parent took up the baton.

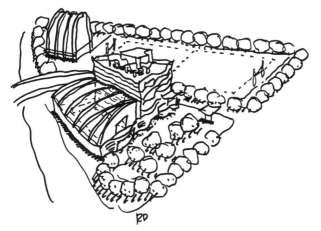

1.14. An early sketch showing the new AquaCenter on the triangular site remaining within the Asphalt Green complex.

1.15. The curves of the AquaCenter's facade link the facility visually to the original parabolic asphalt plant. *Photo © Jeff Goldberg/ESTO.*

1.16. New logo by Donovan & Greene combines the form of the asphalt plant with the waves of the AquaCenter.

1.17. The 50-meter pool and spectator seating are enclosed by a translucent roof supported on soaring, curved steel trusses. *Photo © Jeff Goldberg/ESTO.*

The efforts of certain individuals of unique energy, persistence and wealth have been responsible for many of New York's successful institutions. Rockefeller Center, Rockefeller University, the United Nations Headquarters, Lincoln Center, and the Museum of Modern Art resulted from the efforts of various members of the Rockefeller family and their many friends. The Asphalt Green baton was passed by Dr. Murphy to Al Zesiger, a director of a Wall Street asset management firm. A community resident and parent, avid fitness and swimming enthusiast, Zesiger had long felt that the city lacked a public Olympic-sized pool, and proposed that Asphalt Green build one.

In 1986, Asphalt Green won from the city the right to develop a small triangular site wedged between a public playground, sanitation ramp and the F.D.R. Drive as a pool facility, along with a $4 million matching grant to begin the planning and design. Under Zesiger's direction, over the next seven years the group would contract with the city to operate the new pool, oversee the design of the facility, obtain the many approvals required, and raise over $20 million in additional funds from private schools, individuals and corporations.

The final partnership established would involve three entities in a unique collaboration. New York City would continue to own the park land on which the entire 5-acre Asphalt Green complex sits. Asphalt Green Inc. would contract with the city to operate the facility, at no cost to the city, for a fixed, renewable term. By charging local private schools and individuals user fees and other fund raising, it would staff, operate and maintain the entire complex. A minimum of 30 percent of public use would be at no cost, supported by the fees paid by the 70 percent paid use and other fund raising. The third party participating in this facility would be the Mount Sinai Medical Center, a neighboring hospital which would operate the fourth floor of the new building as The Delacorte Life Center. Essentially a sports and rehabilitation medicine satellite of the hospital, it would complete the full spectrum of sports, fitness and health activities housed in the AquaCenter.

A World-Class Pool

The core of the AquaCenter is a 50-meter, 8-lane Olympic-standard pool with the most sophisticated gutter, lane divider and recirculating system currently available. Built for competition, it can be divided into three swimming zones by floating movable bulkheads. A hydraulic movable floor can vary the depth of one end of the pool from the usual 2 meters to the elevation of the floor deck, where it can extend the deck available for short-course, 25-yard events not requiring the full pool length. Other features include one- and three-meter diving boards, a surge tank to absorb and recirculate overflow, and a large underwater window for observation and instruction.

1.18. The bulge required to accommodate the rectanguar pool (see the plan) has become a design motif for the main facades of the building. *Photo © Jeff Goldberg/ESTO.*

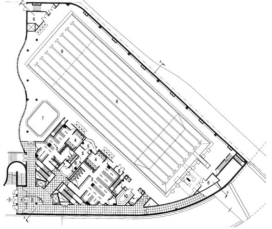

1.19. First Floor Plan: The main pool location on a limited triangular site determined the plan to a large extent.

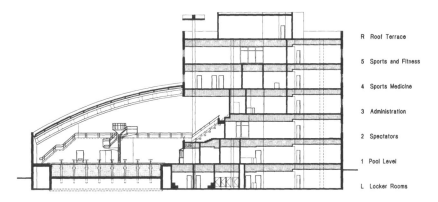

1.20. Section: The curved steel trusses over the main pool echo the parabolic arches of the original asphalt plant structure.

R	Roof Terrace
5	Sports and Fitness
4	Sports Medicine
3	Administration
2	Spectators
1	Pool Level
L	Locker Rooms

1.21. The "waves" of the south and west facades find a counterpoint in the wave-like entrance canopies. *Photo © Jeff Goldberg /ESTO.*

1.22. Second Floor Plan: Spectator seating on this level has a separate entrance from the street, separating "wet" swimmer circulation from "dry" spectator traffic.

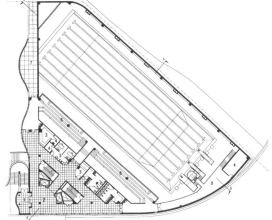

A Place For Everybody

1.23. Waves everywhere. The undulating serpentine walls and waving canopies ameliorate the building's scale and add visual interest. *Photo © Jeff Goldberg/ESTO.*

The success of Asphalt Green and the new AquaCenter points to new possibilities for public improvements by challenging several prevalent assumptions about public facilities:

Public and private sectors have to be completely separate. Although extreme sensitivity is required in making public land and funds available for paid, private use, it is possible to share public facilities to the benefit of both sectors. The agreement between New York City and Asphalt Green gives municipal government the opportunity to monitor both operation and use, insuring public participation in this joint venture. Private funding can multiply the utility of public land, making facilities available which would otherwise not be built.

The rich and the poor can't collaborate. On the contrary, both groups, as well as the majority falling between these extreme economic categories, can work together to their mutual benefit. (I realize that these categories are oversimplifications which can't adequately describe the economic status of an urban population. They are a useful shorthand which helps make a point and were the sub-text of many of the public hearings leading up to the approval of Asphalt Green.) Private school as well as public school kids need swimming facilities and outdoor recreation.

While "rich" residents have the most alternative recreation options, and form the group most able to contribute to a new facility, they also pay a lot of taxes and have a valid claim on public services. "Poor" citizens also pay taxes, and their more limited options give them a more urgent claim on scarce public funding. A project which reaches out to all its natural constituencies can bridge this economic and social gap. For the past 17 years, Asphalt Green has been such a bridge.

Communities resist new public structures. While this is too often the case, a project which promises to serve a wide segment of the community can overcome the inevitable opposition and governmental inertia. It also helps if the proposal replaces a less palatable option (in this case, a large public housing scheme) with a more universally desired facility.

Individuals can't make a difference. They can, and although it obviously helps if they are Rockefellers, Murphys or Zesigers, with their financial resources and social networks, the most important attributes of the individuals who have had an impact on many of the projects in this book have little to do with wealth. These qualities are an immense personal energy and determination, and a deep belief in the importance of their cause.

A project like Asphalt Green is a good deal for everyone involved. The public gains a unique recreation, health and fitness facility, and the donors have the privilege of making a major contribution to our shared environment.

1.24. Waving roof canopies provide shade. Neon lights along the canopy edge are visible from miles away to identify the facility. *Photo © Jeff Goldberg/ESTO.*

1.25. The serpentine west facade forms a soft edge for the children's playground adjoining the AquaCenter. *Photo © Jeff Goldberg/ESTO.*

Higher Goals

1.26. Translucent canopy shelters spectators awaiting entry. *Photo © Roy Wright.*

On a vacant lot in Harlem overgrown with weeds and litter, the artist David Hammons erected a basketball backstop on top of a 40-foot-high pole. A sign in front bears the enigmatic message *"Higher Goals,"* reflecting the contradictory aspects of basketball in the life of young African-American men. As their overwhelmingly favored activity, it is an opportunity for fun and personal accomplishment, and, for a relatively few superbly talented players, a vehicle for success. As an all-consuming pastime in a milieu offering few alternatives, it can also be a diversion from other goals such as education and learning other skills. Seen as a way-station to higher, seemingly unattainable goals, basketball can help boost these players to greater heights.

A block away from Louis Armstrong's home, ELMCOR (a social service organization serving the Elmhurst and Corona neighborhoods in Queens) received a municipal grant for a multi-purpose sports and cultural facility. Joining an existing administrative building and a residence for persons undergoing drug rehabilitation, the Cultural Center houses the larger activity spaces completing the spectrum of facilities offered to this troubled community.

Construction of the Cultural Center formed a unifying, triangular public plaza from which the three ELMCOR facilities are now entered. An abstract sculpture by the artist Howard McCaleb creates a focal point for this urban node. A continuous sheltering canopy along the entire new building enlivens this long facade and protects users from rain and summer sun. By locating the major space at the basement level, the three-story building manages to maintain the low scale of the surrounding residential neighborhood. The "jazzy" facade treatment of diagonal dark brick stripes and orange "rosettes" enlivens the otherwise plain forms of this low-budget building, and pays homage to Louis Armstrong.

1.27. Site Plan: The new Cultural Center completes a complex of three buildings serving the ELMCOR (Elmshurst-Corona) community.

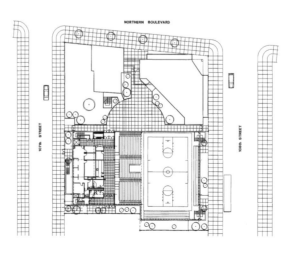

The primary activity space is a two-story competition basketball court with stepped seating for 750 spectators. ELMCOR hosts basketball tournaments of national reputation, and this sport attracts large numbers of participants and viewers. The space can also be used for other sports—volleyball, gymnastics, and martial arts—as well as dance, music and theatrical productions. Other floors house classrooms, an early-childhood center with rooftop recreation, senior citizen activities, arts and crafts shops, and two indoor handball/racquetball courts on the top floor.

1.28. A block from the Louis Armstrong home, a simple facade enlivened by a "jazzy" pattern of diagonal stripes and bright accents. *Photo © Roy Wright.*

1.29. The grand main space is partially below grade to respect the scale of neighborhood residences. *Photo © Roy Wright.*

1.30. Main space is usable for a wide variety of sports, fitness and cultural activities. *Photo © Roy Wright.*

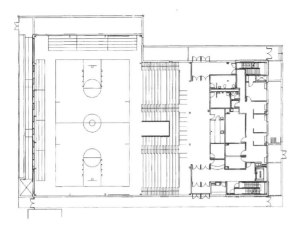

1.31. First Floor Plan: A large multi-purpose space, with seating for 750, houses sports, cultural and social functions.

1.32. The courtyard enclosed by the ELMCOR buildings is at once protected from, and open to, the surrounding streets. *Photo © Roy Wright.*

1.33. Section: Upper levels house classrooms, activity rooms and handball courts. The roof over the main space supports a play terrace.

Civil Rehabilitation

Bellevue Hospital has been caring for New York's sick, elderly, handicapped and injured since 1736. To celebrate its 250th Anniversary, the Bellevue Association commissioned this outdoor training and recreational facility to prepare the physically handicapped, the recovering elderly, the injured athlete, the neurologically disabled, and the hospitalized child for their return to living in the city. The Rehabilitation Park is a safe, scaled-down version of the "real world," with curbs to climb, pot-holes and stairways to navigate, streets to cross, traffic lights, grass, park benches.

The park will encourage its users to safely learn and practice urban survival skills under trained supervision at a pace they can handle. They will practice boarding a real bus, entering an actual taxi, mastering a subway entrance, coping with a house and apartment. These real-life challenges will be supplemented with more recreational rehabilitation—a children's playground, various sports activities, a waterfall and stream, a greenhouse for growing plants and flowers.

Activities and park features offer graduated challenges which accommodate both handicapped and more able users. After mastering as much as they can of the skills challenged in this sheltered workshop for living, park users will be strengthened and more confident as they return to the rigors of daily life in the "real" world.

1.34. A miniature world in which to re-learn life skills.

1.35. A semi-circular loggia will protect outdoor rehabilitation equipment and enclose an elliptical street for learning urban skills.

1.36. A playground will provide safe, protected play for young children with a variety of physical handicaps. The Rusk Institute's Stanton Playground (previously designed by the author) adjoins this facility.

1.38. A city bus and taxi will allow their users to practice without disturbing their fellow passengers.

1.37. This somewhat Utopian plan represents a protected world in miniature. It is an academy for re-learning to navigate the real world outside.

Outdoor Rooms

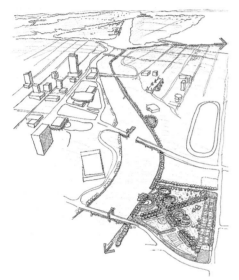

1.39. Tampa's Riverfront Park was envisaged as the first step in a public promenade along the entire frontage of the Hillsborough River.

The predominantly flat topography of this 20-acre site across the Hillsborough River from downtown Tampa, Florida was the setting for a park used by office workers on their lunch hour as well as residents of the adjacent community. Rather than constructing free-standing buildings, the park was designed as a series or earth sculptures—"exterior rooms" carved out of earth berms to preserve the entire park as a green, landscaped surface.

Two diagonal, crossing promenades lined with Eucalyptus trees encourage pedestrian traffic to "short-cut" through the park, resulting in an actively used and therefore safer park. A variety of year-round, day and night activities scheduled for the amphitheater, playing fields and activity circle further draw users to this waterfront location. The planning process for this park included recommendations for extending a public boardwalk along the entire Hillsborough riverfront. A public campaign for private donations has enabled citizens to fund development by "buying" individual planks for this boardwalk. (A similar program in Portland, Oregon, utilized donations for bricks stamped with the donors' names to pave a downtown plaza.)

Enclosed within earth hills of various heights are: an amphitheater; an adventure playground; 10 tennis courts; an outdoor swimming pool; playing fields; and an "activity circle" housing food concessions, public toilets, park storage and maintenance offices under a circular landscaped berm. The interior of this activity space is a paved, landscaped courtyard with a central water fountain surrounded by a colonnade providing shade from the summer sun. Three entrances through the berm are closed at night with roll-down metal grilles.

1.40. Two Eucalyptus shaded paths cross the park, forming the park's armature and encouraging short-cuts through the site.

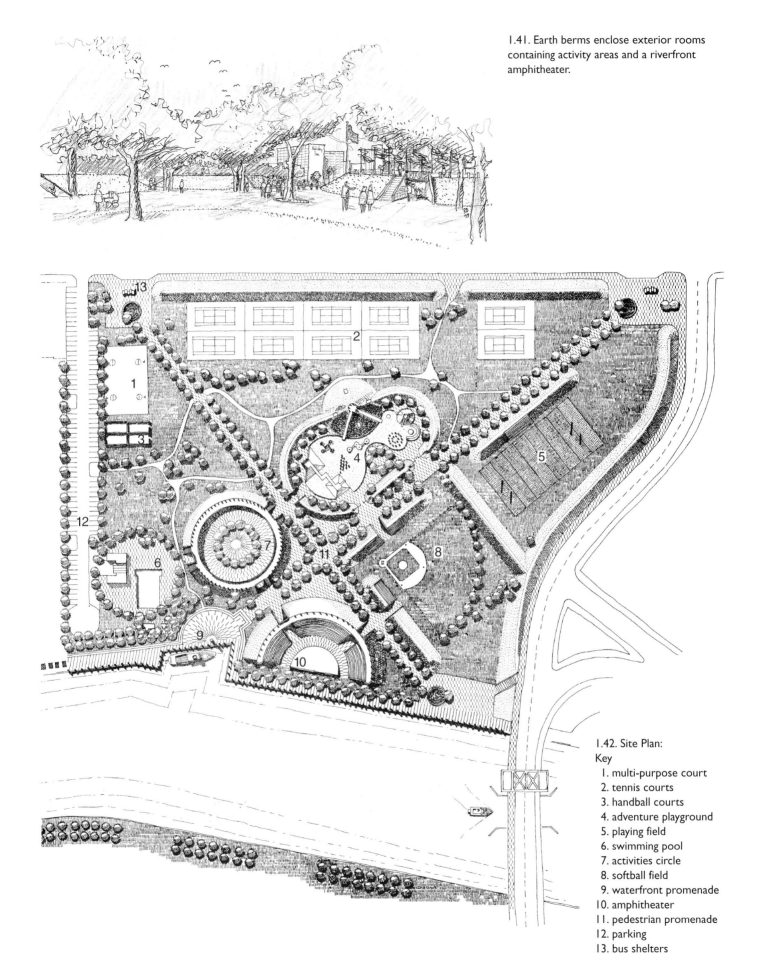

1.41. Earth berms enclose exterior rooms containing activity areas and a riverfront amphitheater.

1.42. Site Plan:
Key
 1. multi-purpose court
 2. tennis courts
 3. handball courts
 4. adventure playground
 5. playing field
 6. swimming pool
 7. activities circle
 8. softball field
 9. waterfront promenade
10. amphitheater
11. pedestrian promenade
12. parking
13. bus shelters

1.43. The main activities circle surrounds an outdoor cafe and water fountain with a protective loggia. Food concessions, service areas and public toilets built into the round berm ring this plaza.

1.44. Earth berms conceal park facilities within a man-made landscape enlivening Tampa's flat topography. Observation walks ring the top of each bermed circle.

1.45. Early conceptual sketch of the activity circle.

1.46. Trellises provide shade for shuffleboard courts.

1.47. The bermed amphitheater is a semicircle facing downtown Tampa across the Hillsborough River.

1.48. Limited entrances into the activity circle allow for enhanced security and simplify closing this area after hours.

Civil Infill

1.49. Filling in the former entrance court creates a community activity space. The original bath house entrances are preserved.

1.50. The original open entrance court in 1936. The new entrance linked the two bath houses to promote year-round use and facilitate supervision. *Photo: Max Ulrich, New York City Parks Photo Archive.*

Typical of the other WPA pools, the Thomas Jefferson Pool in the largely Puerto Rican *barrio* of East Harlem, comprised a girls' and boys' wing formerly entered through a central, open entrance court with a ticket booth. A large outdoor pool and smaller diving pool occupy the space enclosed by these two wings. In cold weather, only the boys' side remained open as a center for amateur boxing. Years of neglected maintenance and water damage had rendered the facility unusable.

The design challenge was to preserve the nobility of the original architecture while rehabilitating the pools and making the facility a year-round recreation center. This was accomplished by filling in the open entrance court to create a new entrance and large community meeting room and to link the two wings. The gently bowed main facade introduces formal variety while respecting the original design, materials, and detailing.

During the swimming season, boys and girls line up and enter directly through the locker and shower areas in the two wings, thus simplifying circulation during this busiest usage. Separating boys from girls in these entrance lines also facilitates supervision and reduces anti-social behavior. In the off-season, the wing entrances are closed and all users arrive through the staffed central entrance. Connecting the wings internally means that both locker rooms can be used for a variety of indoor activities, boxing, martial arts, weight lifting, dance and aerobics.

The large swimming pool was restored by constructing a new stainless steel wall and recirculating gutter system inside the existing concrete walls. The existing concrete pool floor was repaired and existing pipe tunnels were used to house a new circulation and filtration system. The community and Parks Department agreed that the former diving pool was dangerous given the limited instruction and supervision that would be available. This deep pool was filled in, reducing its depth to create a wading pool for the many community children too young to use the main pool. Wading and swimming pools are separated by a low fence to keep young children away from the larger pool. (The Riverbank State Park pool, pp. 56–57, has a similar arrangement.)

Some of the larger outdoor pools in New York have lately experienced widely publicized events where large numbers of boys surrounded a girl, frightening or sexually harassing her. The vast size of these WPA pools makes it difficult for lifeguards to quickly spot and prevent this behavior. One solution currently under study would divide these pools by floating bulkheads into smaller, more easily manageable areas.

1.51. The new curved facade incorporates original materials, scale and detailing to create an invisible seam between old and new.

1.52. The stepped facade and skylight monitors modulate this facade, express the three pools within, and echo the forms of the Rocky Mountains to the west. *Photo © Jerry Butts.*

1.53. This large, greenhouse-like space houses three pools on multiple levels with a variety of slides, waterfalls and fountains. The deep, upper level pool has platform diving, rope swings and a curved slide to the middle pool. *Photo © Jerry Butts.*

City Park Recreation Center, Westminster, Colorado: *Barker Rinker Seacat & Partners Architects.* One of several new "super" centers in the Denver area built with public funds and supported by user fees. Serving as community centers, they provide child care, health clinics and other social services in addition to recreation.

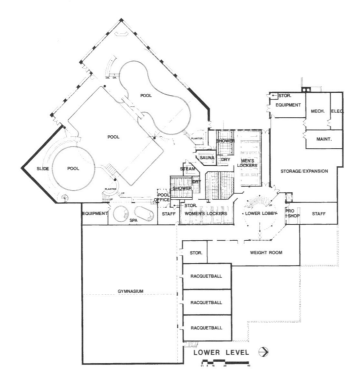

1.54. Lower Level Plan: Lockers, weight rooms, racquetball courts, gymnasium and leisure pool are on this level.

Central Park Zoo, New York City: *Kevin Roche John Dinkeloo and Associates Architects.* A new zoo fashioned out of the old zoo originally built during the WPA. The formal garden at the center was retained, as were four of the original buildings. A colonnade unifies the entire composition of buildings and natural areas into a gentle order of wonderful scale and beauty, a Jeffersonian balance between gardens and buildings.

1.55. Brick and granite columns support the wood and glass trellis now covered with vines. The interior formal garden was carefully restored and a new sea lion pool created, updating a much-loved New York landmark. *Photo © KRJDA.*

1.56. Nature frames an octagonal window framing nature beyond in this place of calmness and balance. *Photo © KRJDA.*

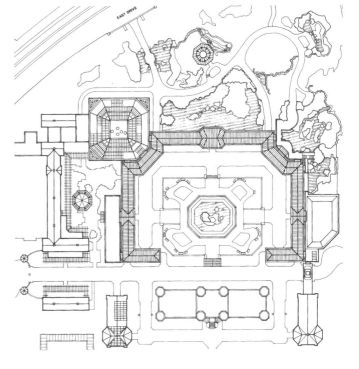

1.57. Site Plan: A cloistered colonnade, nature within and without. Animals live in conditions that duplicate their natural habitats as closely as possible, and observers (and animals) are kept safe by natural barriers.

1.58. Scale, massing, and materials of the stadium enclosure reinforce the surrounding urban context. *Photo © Jeff Goldberg/ESTO.*

Oriole Park, Baltimore, MD. *HOK Sports Group Architects, HOK/RTKL/Wallace, Roberts & Todd, Master Planners.* Reversing a long trend, Oriole Park reinforces its urban context and celebrates both the sport and the city. A restored railroad warehouse beyond right field provides an enclosure and establishes the materials of the new stadium. Along with the new Buffalo stadium (by the same group), this facility restores some of the old magic of baseball.

1.59. Landscaped promenade between the railroad warehouse and right field leads to the parking fields. The 1911 Bromo-Seltzer tower dominates the local skyline. *Photo © Jeff Goldberg/ESTO.*

Riverbank State Park
Case Study

2

Architectural Triage (Civil Limitations)

Having become increasingly aware of a link between the work of architects and physicians, let me borrow a medical term to propose a strategy for making design decisions in a world of limited resources. Triage, a system of assigning priorities of medical treatment based on urgency or chance of survival, is a term usually applied on battlefields or in hospital emergency rooms. One treats first those in the most extreme circumstances who have a chance for survival, then those less afflicted who will survive, last, those with little or no chance of survival. In a world of unlimited resources this would be a cruel policy. In a world of severely limited possibilities it is an approach suggesting the allocation of scarce resources to help the largest number with the most enduring effect.

Architects of public work, like public servants, deal in the art of the possible. We also labor in a realm of choices, priorities, and the determination of what will yield the greatest good for the greatest number. We practice architectural triage.

2

Riverbank State Park
Case Study

2.1. Location Plan: The North River Pollution Treatment Facility supporting Riverbank State Park treats sewage from most of the west side of Manhattan.

There are public facilities which are usually invisible unless something is wrong, or we live next to them. We wash our dishes, take a bath, and flush the toilet without a further thought about the destination of the effluent and its effect on our shared environment. For the early years of Manhattan's settlement, it didn't matter that much of its sewage was flowing, untreated, into the Hudson River. As population, industry, and public awareness grew, it began to matter very much. In 1965, a Federal Court issued an order requiring New York City to treat all its remaining raw sewage before discharging it, and a search began for a suitable site along Manhattan's Hudson river front.

Early Phases, 1967–1979

Several sites were studied and rejected because of intense community opposition and political pressure. In 1968, a site was finally selected at the western edge of the Harlem community, between West 137th and West 145th Streets. This decision resulted in 25 years of community protest, political struggle, and a variety of efforts to assuage the community by balancing the pain of locating a sewage plant in its front yard with the benefits possible from its construction.

Public works of this magnitude normally set aside a portion of their construction budget for "beautification"—visual amenities enhancing their presence in a community. To provide this beauty, a silk purse *on* a sow's ear, Philip Johnson was commissioned in 1968 to lend his considerable talent and reputation to the efforts of the plant's engineers. He proposed a grand scheme—Plan No. 1—flooding the 28-acre roof of the plant to create a vast reflecting pool from which a series of fountains would gush. Renderings and an elaborate scale model were prepared for presentation to the community. The pool and fountains, it was repeatedly explained to rising derision, were most definitely *not effluent*; they used clean, New York City water. The local outcry was intense, leading to the 1969 decision by Governor Nelson Rockefeller to construct a state park on the roof of the proposed sewage plant.

The architectural firm of Gruzen & Partners was retained to prepare a master plan for the newly named Riverbank State Park consistent with a goal of maximizing possible recreation uses on the plant roof and on the adjacent river front. This Plan No. 2 of 1969 was responsive to both the recreation needs of the affected neighborhood and the special problems and opportunities of this unique site. The essential issue of access (the site is located 400 feet from Riverside Drive and 58 feet above ground level, requiring bridging across a railroad right-of-way and the six-lane Henry Hudson Parkway) was addressed by extending a two-block-wide platform from Riverside Park to the plant roof.

2.2. Postcard of San Francisco's Sutro Baths circa 1900; an early prototype of an enclosed urban recreation facility. *Photo © Cliff House.*

The platform itself was to be landscaped, and would form a base for several park buildings. At the north and south ends of the plant, the roof would terrace down to the level of the surrounding land, creating a link facilitating the future development of the entire riverfront.

Community opposition lessened considerably, although factions continued to oppose the project in the belief that if the Park could be stopped the treatment plant would be similarly abandoned, a strategy that was to continue for many years despite the massive construction activities clearly visible at the site. Plan No. 2 was shelved largely because the cost of the bridging platform and linking terraces brought the total cost far beyond the State's funding ability.

At that time, and at subsequent periods when the full realization of the scale of this proposed undertaking was confronted by government, alternate strategies were investigated in an attempt to control costs: the "no-build" option (part of the jargon of environmental assessments required for projects of this scale, it translates as "do nothing, leave it alone"); the option of enhancing several nearby public parks instead of building Riverbank; the option of granting the community a lump sum to spend for a public improvement of its choice.

2.3. Panoramic view of Riverbank from an adjoining building. To the north are the Palisades, the George Washington Bridge and views 20 miles up the Hudson; to the south are views of New York Harbor and the midtown skyline; to the west is New Jersey. *Photo © Norman McGrath.*

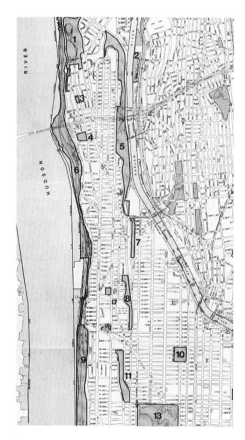

2.4. Existing parks in Upper Manhattan: Most existing parks are located along the edges of the community and are either undeveloped or not easily accessible.

2.5. Plan by Gruzen & Partners in 1969: The connection between the proposed park and community was an almost three-block-wide platform supporting the main park buildings. *Drawing: Courtesy of Gruzen Samton Architects.*

The "no-build" choice was clearly unacceptable to the community—the plant would be built with no compensating amenities to make up for the expected 25 years of construction and the permanent presence of a sewage plant on their riverfront. The option of distributing benefits around the neighborhood was not acceptable to those residents closest to the plant, who expected benefits commensurate with their greater pain. Community representatives also feared that distributed benefits would disappear into a City park system already unable to properly maintain its current inventory of open space—the State Park would, at least, be maintained with State funds, and expenditures would be easier to monitor.

Pressure was also building to replace the selected architect with a minority firm which would, in the community's opinion, be more responsive to their special requirements. In 1973, the firms of Bond Ryder & Associates and Lawrence Halprin Associates, were retained to design the Park again. Their Plan No. 3 went further in meeting the recreation needs identified by community representatives, providing swimming pools, skating facilities, athletic buildings, playing fields, and educational facilities. Megastructures housing these functions extended along the eastern perimeter of the plant roof, blocking traffic noise from the adjoining highway, but also creating a potential visual barrier to views from Riverside Drive and the apartment buildings lining it. The roof was to be filled with four feet of soil to create a new ground level which would be extensively landscaped.

Left unresolved were the ever-increasing estimated construction costs, both to construct the elaborate design and to uniformly strengthen the plant's roof to support the structures, soil cover, and landscaping—costs estimated in 1978 as approaching $250 million (easily twice that figure in 1993 dollars).

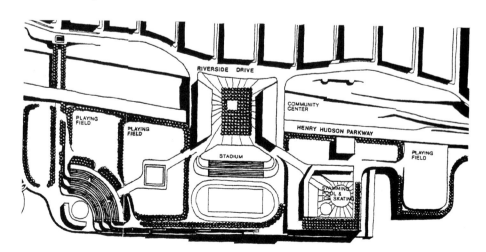

Another impasse loomed, with the community strongly demanding what they felt was due them, and the State (now joined by Federal and City representatives) balking at the increasing costs.

By now, the sewage plant was under construction, with large caissons being sunk over 150 feet through the river and its mud bottom to the bedrock below. If a park was to be built at all, this foundation would have to be reinforced to support the park's weight in addition to the weight of the plant, the plant's contents, and the weight of the caissons themselves. Additional time pressures were being applied by the courts. In 1979, the Federal, State and City governments entered into a consent decree (a court-ordered implementation plan with the force of law) requiring the sewage plant to be in operation by 1987, with heavy fines for non-compliance. Late in 1979, Plan No. 3 was abandoned and 12 firms invited to submit their qualifications to prepare Plan No. 4.

Design and Redesign, 1980–1989

Architect selection was by a committee of State officials and community representatives with a variety of concerns and goals: community residents wanted a firm, preferably minority-owned, which would attend to the community's need for meaningful participation in determining recreation needs and securing local employment during the construction and subsequent staffing of the Park; government officials wanted a firm with the technical capability to design a park which *could be built*, within a budget which seemed increasingly inadequate, and that could balance responsiveness to community demands with responsibility for the exigencies of construction. The selection process was difficult and acrimonious. The author's firm, with its consultant team members for landscape architecture, structural and mechanical engineering, was selected on the basis of a compromise between the factions.

Planning Phase, 1978–1980

Planning began with an almost clean slate, upon which was written "$51 million," the funding then available to build the Park and its access bridges. Over the next year, there were meetings every other week with a Steering Committee of community residents, local elected officials, and representatives from the major Federal, State and City agencies which would oversee, construct, pay for, and, ultimately, operate Riverbank State Park. The design team inventoried existing parks and recreation facilities, defined public transportation opportunities, studied adjoining community facilities and land-use patterns, identified local demographics, and studied the technical limits to construction at this difficult location.

2.6. Aerial photograph from the north illustrates Riverbank State Park's relationship to Manhattan and the Hudson River. *Photo © Julian Olivas.*

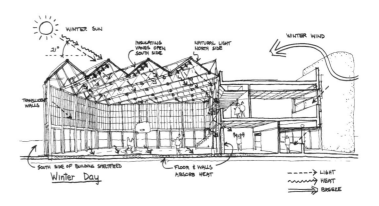

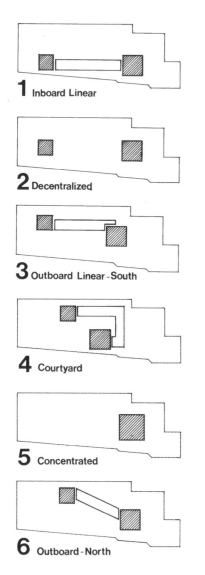

1 Inboard Linear

2 Decentralized

3 Outboard Linear–South

4 Courtyard

5 Concentrated

6 Outboard–North

2.7. Conceptual drawings of the six design approaches for the park which were presented to the community steering group and formed the basis of subsequent discussion.

Program Development

First came the development of a program, a list of activities and spaces which would be provided in the Park. Discussions, while free-ranging, were kept within the framework of available funding, technical requirements, and social realities. An overly expensive feature (a large swimming pool with artificial waves was favored by several participants) would require losing several more modest facilities. A pool deep enough to permit diving could not be supported on the plant roof, and diving was considered by many a dangerous activity. The program developed as part of the Facility Plan of August, 1980, would become the "bible" defining the Park's requirements and proposed facilities for the next 13 years.

At the end of this fact-finding and programming phase, design options were generated for consideration, beginning with the access bridges. Five locations were evaluated, and two ultimately selected by the Committee: a 50-foot-wide, two-lane vehicular bridge with a wide pedestrian walkway at West 145th Street; and a 40-foot-wide, single-lane bridge for emergency vehicles and pedestrians at West 138th Street. The Park would thus be accessible at both ends of its nine-block length, convenient to public access by way of the 145th Street crosstown bus, and the West 145th and West 137th Street subway stations on Broadway, one block east of Riverside Drive. To create a link to the City park to the north, a stair and elevator tower would be provided. Although some on the Committee wanted bridges at every cross street, and others wanted no bridges on *their* street, compromise prevailed. So far, so good!

Community participants, once they were accepted into the decision-making process, became generally cooperative, although resentments over the treatment plant lingered. The plant continued under construction, while the construction of the Park which would compensate for the plant's deficits was many years away. The Park project was seen by some as a trick to divert the community's attention from the problems anticipated when the plant began operation—the possibility of smells and air pollution, and a feared potential of explosion from methane gas generated in the sewage treatment process. To separate these issues, committee meetings now began to be organized in two parts, the first to discuss the plant and its design, the second to continue evaluating design alternatives for the Park.

Six conceptual schemes for the park were now presented to the Committee, together with a list of *Design Criteria* against which these schemes could be evaluated and ranked, including: protection from north wind; orientation to the sun and energy conservation; proximity to access points; flexibility of use; views of the river from the proposed buildings; preservation of views from surrounding buildings; screening out highway noise and views; ability to zone for seasonal use; ease of supervision and operation; and the security of Park users. The Committee and design team ranked the six schemes against the design goals and assigned numerical scores.

2.8. The original roof design for park buildings (left) consisted of continuous skylights angled to maximize passive solar heating in winter. This intricate structure was modified toward the end of the design process.

2.9. Conceptual sketch (right) showing how summer sun would be excluded while winter sun was allowed to penetrate the building. The energy crisis provided a powerful, but short-lived, impetus to energy-efficient initiatives by public agencies.

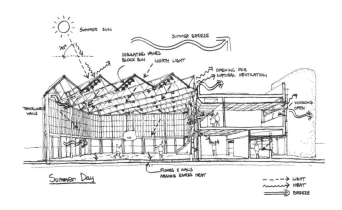

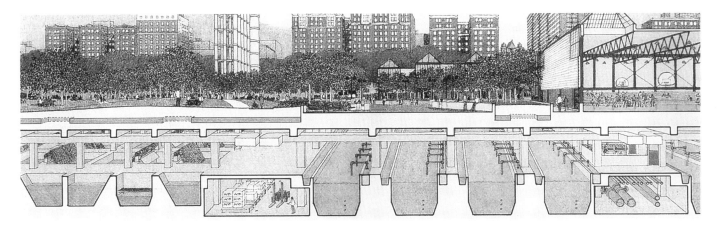

The two highest-ranked conceptual designs were selected for further development and more detailed design, and were presented at a large public hearing with renderings, plans and scale models. After evaluating comments from this hearing, the Committee selected one alternative as most closely meeting their needs. With some minor modifications, the design selected was the one eventually built, although not without continuing crises in the 13 years remaining until construction was completed. Later that year, the team was instructed to begin detailed plans and working drawings for the construction of the Park.

2.10. Exploded view of the sewage plant showing the treatment functions contained in the almost half-mile-long building supporting Riverbank. *Drawing: A.C. Bergmann.*

Design and Redesign, 1980–1989

The construction cost estimates of 1980 had been predicated on receiving a proportion (3½ percent) of the cost of the plant to supplement the $24 million State contribution. The plant was now redesigned, reducing its cost (and the Park's share) while a steep inflation of construction costs began to raise the Park's cost. Like passengers in a sinking balloon, the project began to shed excess baggage. The original designs of the building's roofs included sophisticated, angled skylights with light-actuated shades which would exclude the hot sun of summer, welcome sunlight on winter days, and insulate the buildings against cold, winter nights. The angling of these continuous skylights, planned to provide the optimum orientation to the sun, was technically intricate and expensive and became the first design feature to be modified to reduce costs. The redesigned roofs now featured simpler roof trusses and skylights at right angles.

A marketing study suggested that the two-story restaurant was too large for the probable market, and the restaurant was redesigned to a one-story structure with a large outdoor terrace for summer dining. At the request of the New York State Department of Transportation, the access bridges were redesigned to make periodic safety inspections simpler, also resulting in a more cost-effective structure.

**Riverbank State Park
Case Study**

2.11. The protective screening required to protect state highways was turned into a decorative feature of the two access bridges.

Value Engineering

These redesigns were accomplished in a process called "value engineering," a procedure increasingly adopted to control costs on large-scale public projects. Comparable to a medical second opinion, value engineering typically involves a week of continuous meetings among the project's sponsors, architects and engineers, and a team of outside value engineers (a recent profession in this age of specialization) who question every basic assumption, design strategy, and technical solution in the project to date. Ranging from the most general questions (Is this project necessary? Could it be accomplished another way?) to the most specific (Could ceramic tile be eliminated from the bathrooms?), the various decisions made to that date are questioned, priced both as to present costs and long-term ("life-cycle") costs, and exhaustively debated. The process is usually difficult and often contentious, as competing interests vie for the soul of the project: initial cost versus life-cycle cost, durability versus the cost of materials, architectural character and design versus the bottom line. The value engineers are retained to cut costs, and they attack on all fronts to accomplish this goal, which is usually the goal of the funding agency as well.

Architects since the time of Vitruvius (author of the *Ten Books of Architecture* in the First Century B.C.) have striven to provide *commodity, firmness and delight*. While the first two are suitable subjects for objective analysis by value engineers and bean (beam?) counters, *delight*, that most subtle of categories embracing much of what distinguishes inspired architecture from junk, is difficult to value—it is worth nothing, or everything. To that which yields *delight* in a building, value engineers can only respond as a courtly patron did to Mozart after hearing him perform, "Too many notes, Mozart!" (Mozart's reply was reputedly, "Just as many as are required!")

That said, fairness requires that the positive aspects of the value engineering process be acknowledged: an outside evaluation can help to reconfirm intelligent decisions and revise foolish ones; it can clarify for the operating agency (in this case, New York State Parks) the long-term costs of maintaining a facility; it provides another check on the expenditure of public funds. Since these tasks can best be performed at an early phase in the project, value engineering typically takes place at the end of the schematic and/or design development phases. For Riverbank, a period of inflation required values to be engineered at several stages of the project's development, requiring intricate and time-consuming revisions to hundreds of drawings. Over a year was spent making these changes, resulting in savings of approximately $8 million. In the spring of 1987, almost nine years since the beginning of the design phase, construction finally started on the first phase of Riverbank State Park.

48   Civil Architecture

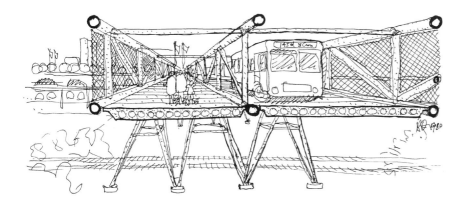

2.12. These originally designed space-frame bridges were replaced by designs simpler to inspect and maintain.

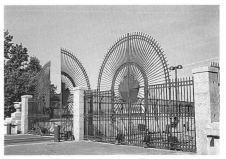

2.14. Decorative entrance gates supported on granite piers integrate the new park into the Olmsted-designed Riverside Park.

2.13. The standard components of highway bridges—concrete piers and steel beams— are here utilized to create a curving, welcoming pedestrian approach to the park. Only emergency vehicles, handicapped access transport and the public bus may use the access bridges.

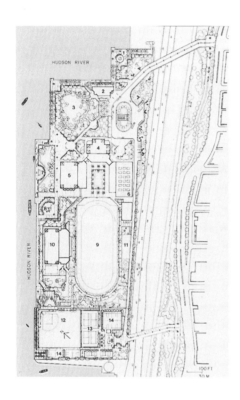

**Riverbank State Park,
New York City**
1. Carousel
2. Restaurant
3. Picnic area
4. Cultural building
5. Athletic building
6. Skating rink
7. Amphitheater
8. Playground
9. Football field
10. Swimming pool
11. Community gardens
12. Softball fields
13. Tennis courts
14. Basketball courts

2.15. Site plan of the completed park: The 28-acre plant roof supporting the park consists of 14 independently moving plates which limited the location of the park structures.

Construction and Redesign, 1987–1993

As the design study had begun with issues of access to the park, construction began on the two access bridges and the stair and elevator tower. By this time, the plant roof which would support the park was only finished at the north end of the plant, with the remaining roof areas still under construction. The $35 million first construction phase could therefore only include two of the smaller park buildings—the restaurant and carousel over the completed plant. After watching construction of the plant for 20 years, community residents could now see the first portions of the long-promised park becoming real.

The Steering Committee visited the site, elected officials started taking credit for their years of effort in preserving project funds, and Riverbank was about to become, in New York parlance, "a done deal," when two situations which had been developing for some time surfaced to public awareness. The plant smelled, and continuing inflation made the park's funding again insufficient to build the now value-engineered design.

The plant, although not fully completed, had begun treating sewage, a fact immediately apparent by an unmistakable odor on certain warm days when river breezes wafted toward the neighboring apartment buildings. Plant operators claimed that the smell came from improper operation or minor spills, but community residents insisted that the smells were pervasive and possibly unhealthy. Community meetings once again turned angry, and this situation worsened as a $20 million shortfall appeared in the now $148 million cost of the park. With part of the park already under construction, a final round of cost reductions would be required, in the face of a community angry over broken government promises and a *New York Times* editorial titled "The North River Plant Still Stinks."

At the end of 1989, the New York State Office of General Services (the construction agency responsible for much of the state's construction) was asked to take over the construction of Riverbank. Still remaining was the cost differential between available funding and project cost.

In a period of two weeks, a redesign was prepared for the remaining portions of the park which preserved the floor plans and program requirements of the original design while maintaining the architectural character of the buildings and landscaped areas. This proposal would save $20 million by eliminating the roof over the skating rink, simplifying the roofs of all the buildings, substituting metal wall panels for translucent walls, and replacing an elevated, enclosed walkway between the gymnasium and swimming pool buildings with a simpler, covered walkway.

By the end of 1990, the design of the park as it would be built was completed, with an optional arched roof over the skating rink designed

and bid as an alternate in the event that low bids yielded additional funds. By that year, construction trades in New York City had entered into a serious recession and the final phases of Riverbank were awarded $5 million below expectations, allowing the skating rink to be covered and other features to be restored.

Riverbank State Park was dedicated by Governor Mario Cuomo on May 27, 1993, 15 years after the design team joined the project and 24 years after having first been announced by Governor Rockefeller. In the first year of Riverbank's operation, 3 million visitors flocked to the park, making it the second most visited facility (after Jones Beach) in the State Park system.

2.16. View of the all-weather playing field: Over 80 percent of the park is landscaped for a variety of active and passive outdoor activities. The built park gives users the experience of boarding a vast, floating structure permanently moored to the Manhattan shore. *Photo © Norman McGrath.*

2.17. Two elevator and stair towers link the upper-level park to grade and river elevations. This view shows the tower providing access to the platform containing the river-front amphitheater. The lower-level amphitheater has spectacular river views and is located far from the surrounding residential streets to minimize disturbance from performance events. *Photo © Norman McGrath.*

The Built Park, 1993

The 28-acre plant roof, almost a half-mile long, consists of 14 separate sections moving independently as the roof expands and contracts due to changes in temperature, like the scales of a giant armadillo along the water's edge. Each roof plate can support a different load depending on the column spacing below, up to a maximum of 400 pounds per square foot. Park buildings must be supported within individual roof plates (to avoid damage from movement at expansion joints) with every park building column located directly over a corresponding plant column below.

The entire park—buildings, landscaping, site features—is on a strict diet because of the limited load-bearing capacity of the plant's caissons, columns and roof spans. Deducting from those capacities the expected live loads (people, vehicles, snow) yielded the allowable weight of the buildings, retaining walls, soil, trees, and pavement. Buildings could only be lightweight steel structures with metal or tile-faced panels, and areas of

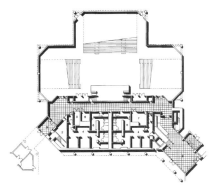

2.18. Cultural Building Plan. In each building a two-story wing of ancillary rooms adjoins the large main space.

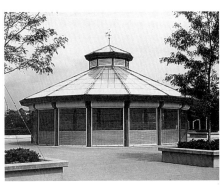

2.19. The carousel provides a welcoming sight, and sound, for park users arriving over the West 145th Street bridge. *Photo © Stanley Greenberg.*

2.20. The entire skating rink and the corners of the other park buildings open to the outdoors to exploit the views and breezes of this unique location. *Photo © Norman McGrath.*

deep soil required to support large plantings were lightened by a honeycomb of Styrofoam panels (made without ozone-depleting CFC's).

The design of the required utilities was similarly difficult as most of the pipes, drains, and electrical conduits had to run over (rather than under) the plant roof. Finally, the park had to be constructed without affecting either the remaining construction of the plant or its operation. While none of these design limits are apparent, they had a profound effect on every aspect of the built structures.

The selected conceptual design organized the four largest park buildings around a south-facing courtyard sheltered from winter winds. Skating rink, multi-purpose cultural building, and gymnasium are linked by enclosed passageways. The swimming pool is reachable by a covered walkway to facilitate circulation in bad weather. Because it would be many years between the planning and realization of Riverbank, and it was expected that community demographics and recreation priorities would change, maximum program flexibility was designed into each building.

2.21. Riverbank's main lobby is a point of orientation from which much of the park is visible and elevator access provided to the upper level. *Photo © Norman McGrath.*

Restaurant and Carousel. As the first structure seen when arriving over the West 145th Street bridge, the carousel's color, movement, and music are meant to establish a friendly mood, inviting to children and adults alike. The restaurant is sited to take advantage of views north to the George Washington Bridge and the New Jersey Palisades. In warm weather a large terrace is opened for outdoor dining and a snack bar served by the restaurant kitchen is available. For the infrequent days when a plant malfunction might release unwanted smells, an odor suppressing ventilation system has been installed. To encourage restaurant use in winter and after park hours, a parking area has been located below the Henry Hudson Parkway with an elevator providing a convenient connection.

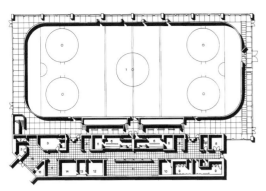

2.22. Skating Rink Plan: The skating rink shed encloses an ice-skating facility for six months a year, and roller skating for the remaining period. A skate shop, concession stand, and lockers are housed in the attached wing, the roof of which serves as a viewing terrace.

2.23. Covered walkway links swimming building with other recreational structures. *Photo © Norman McGrath.*

Cultural Building. The required flexibility is here provided by a large space with three wings radiating from a central stage area. Bleachers in these wings can be retracted or extended to create performance spaces for music, film, dance, theater or gymnastics. The two-story portion contains backstage dressing rooms, lockers, storage, and administrative offices for the park.

Skating Facility. Originally planned to be enclosed, then as an open rink to reduce costs, the built facility is a fortunate compromise, a curved shed roof protecting the rink from sun, rain and snow, and open to the air on four sides. To conserve energy and reflect seasonal interests, an ice surface will be maintained from late fall to early spring, with a concrete roller-skating surface available during warmer seasons. A single-story wing houses lockers, skate rentals, and a food concession area, while its roof is utilized as a viewing terrace.

2.24. The indoor 50-meter pool can be divided into three pool areas by two movable bulkheads, allowing competitive swimming, warm-up, and instruction to take place simultaneously. *Photo © Norman McGrath.*

2.25. Park buildings are designed as flexible, multi-purpose enclosures which accommodate changing recreation priorities. *Photo © Norman McGrath.*

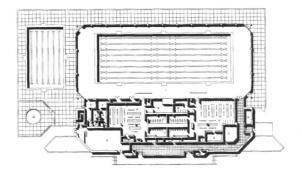

2.26. Swimming Pool Plan: Locker facilities on the pool level allow convenient handicapped accessibility. Outdoor 25-yard pool shares use of indoor lockers and toilets.

Swimming Pools. An enclosed 50-meter pool is divided by two movable bulkheads, which can be deployed at one end for 50-meter competitive swimming or arranged to simultaneously create three pool areas for recreational swimming, instruction and 25-yard competitive events. Lifts provide handicapped accessibility. In warm weather, an outdoor 25-yard pool, wading pool, and large surrounding terraces supplement the indoor facility. The swimming complex has been located close to the river to take advantage of the summer breezes and to give swimmers and sun-bathers spectacular views of the Hudson River Palisades to the north.

Athletic Building. Designed as a flexible container for the widest possible range of indoor athletic activities, this facility comprises a large, divisible gymnasium adjoining a two-story wing containing exercise rooms, classrooms, lockers and other activity areas. Wide corridor windows allow passers-by to see the activities in the gym to invite their involvement as spectators and participants.

2.27. Corner skylight pyramids provide natural light to building interiors and punctuate the exterior corners of the park buildings. At night, they glow softly along the Henry Hudson Parkway. *Photo © Norman McGrath.*

2.28. A continuous promenade rings the
entire park, providing seating, shade trees, and
a sea-rail design which has become standard
for much of Manhattan's waterfront. *Photo ©
Norman McGrath.*

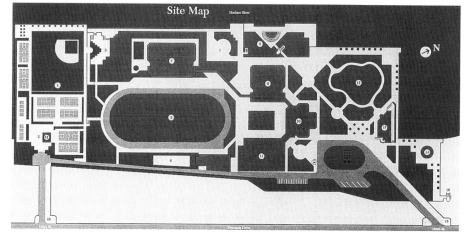

2.29. Site Map and Park Rules: From park
graphics and a NYSOPRHP pamphlet
designed by Anthony Russell.

2.30. A 2½-acre platform at the river's edge is exploited to provide a boat landing, fishing and an outdoor amphitheater. Access to the river's edge is by a stair and elevator tower. *Photo © Norman McGrath.*

Riverbank State Park

679 Riverside Drive (at West 145th Street)
Park Hours: 6 am - 11 pm
Information: (212) 694-3600

Rules and regulations

- Children under 10 years of age must be accompanied by a person 18 years or older.
- Drinking alcoholic beverages is not permitted.
- Smoking is prohibited in: Park buildings, pool areas, children's play areas and in field sports areas.
- Open fires and cooking prohibited.
- Dogs and pets are not allowed.
- No public parking.

The use and enjoyment of Riverbank State Park is governed by the rules and regulations of the New York State Office of Parks, Recreation and Historic Preservation, Parts 370 through 378, Title 9, and other applicable statutes and codes.

Facilities available at the park

1 Playing Fields
   Softball
   Basketball
   Handball/Paddleball
   Office
   Tennis
2 Childrens Playground
3 Water Play Area
4 Swimming Pools
5 Running Track
   Football/Soccer Field
6 Community Garden
   Greenhouse

7 Children's Playground
8 Waterfront Amphitheatre
9 Athletic Building
   Police Base
10 Cultural Center
11 Skating Rink
12 Picnic Area
13 Riverbank Cafe
   Snack Bar
14 Carousel
15 To Public Transportation
16 North Stair Tower & Elevator

♿ Park buildings and facilities are accessible to persons with disabilities

How to get to the Park

Pedestrian Access: Riverbank State Park is located on the Hudson River between West 137th Street and West 145th Street in Manhattan. Two park entrance bridges span from Riverside Drive over the Henry Hudson Parkway to the rooftop park. At West 145th Street, access is also available from the lower riverfront level of Riverside Park via stairs or an elevator.

By Subway: Westside IRT local # 9 "skip stop" service to West 145th Street. Walk one block west to the park.

By Bus: Bronx Crosstown BX19 West to Riverbank or to Broadway & West 145th Street. Walk west on West 145th Street one block to the park. This bus will provide direct service into the park between the hours of 7 am and 11 pm. **Or take** alternate bus route of your choice to Broadway and 145th Street.

2.31. View of the Cultural Building and
Athletic Building from the main entrance walk
leading from the West 145th Street bridge to
the lookout over the Hudson River and the
elevator and stair tower to the lower-level
river landing. *Photo © Norman McGrath.*

Public Schools

3

We Know Too Much (Civil Overload)

A modern, literate, urban-dwelling adult in an industrialized nation (i.e., an architect or student of architecture in the U.S.) has access to an amount of information which would have been incomprehensible to a comparable individual living a century earlier. We are overwhelmed with data (much of it unsubstantiated), images (many of great beauty and trivial import, attempting to sell us products of dubious necessity), news (much of it new only in the identity of the latest victims of an apparently static sequence of human tragedy—fire, crime, famine, war). In every area of our lives, we know (see and hear) more about more, but know (understand) less, and can do less about it. Explain, if you can, the tangled, tragic history of the Serbs, Bosnians and Croats.

This information overload poses special difficulties for practitioners and students of architecture. Students are attempting creative, original first-time solutions to design problems. Where once they had the leisure to learn a single approach under a few teachers and practitioners, learning by imitation and trial and error, they are now exposed to everything at once. The gap between students' fledgling abilities and their concurrent awareness of the work of "star" architects—whose work gains the widest publication—too often leads to feelings of inadequacy, a professional "fear of flying." Who to emulate? How to trust one's perception and instinct in the face of the more developed talent of countless others?

For a practitioner the problem becomes more difficult and subtle: How to avoid the twin traps of either uncritically appropriating the "ism" of the moment (post-modernism, deconstructivism, etc.) or establishing an instantly recognizable "signature style." Both are often rewarded but equally often lead to creative dead ends, the first by avoiding original thinking, the second by encouraging endless repetition of the ideas which brought the architect original success.

3   Public Schools

"Nowhere does an architect have a better chance to display his skill than in the planning of school buildings, and nowhere does he perform a job of greater importance for the public welfare." (Talbot Hamlin, "Schools are for Children," *Pencil Points,* March 1939.)

Until relatively recently, public schools were the glue that held together our shared culture. Or, rather, schools manufactured a civilizing substance which would stick to the busy creatures entering their hives of learning, and be taken home by them in the afternoon, thus promoting the assimilation of families and immigrant groups into a common culture. Along with that process, some reading, writing and arithmetic would also be absorbed. Civilization was Lesson #1, the other subjects followed.

Since the late 1960s, disagreements about which glue, if any, is the appropriate binder for an increasingly diverse, multicultural society, have called into question the entire enterprise of public education. Out of choice or perceived necessity, many now choose private schools, parochial schools, or military academies to transmit their special version of the shared culture to their children. This fragmentation has also permeated the public school realm, where special education schools, magnet schools, schools for gifted students, alternative schools, and academies focusing on specialized curricula proliferate. In a recent development, private companies are contracting to take over public schools, possibly improve their performance, and try to make a profit doing it.

Schools as Civilizers

Although this is not the place for a protracted discussion about the present state of public education, a personal belief is offered: public education, with all its problems, is an essential component of a civil, democratic society. The alternative, now visible all around us, is the increasing Balkanization of our society along ethnic, racial and class divisions. The individual cultures from which we derive much of our identity are diminished without the shared common language and culture necessary for civil discourse and coexistence.

As noted in the introduction to this book, the public school experience of this writer mirrors that of countless others, then and now. In a period of nine years, having arrived in New York City a Spanish-speaking nine-year-old, three public schools and two public high schools provided sufficient security and sustenance to produce a reasonably acculturated and educated candidate for higher education and civil adulthood, by no means a small task. With public support, adequate funding and improved facilities, public schools can continue to accomplish this vital task.

3.1. The little school on the prairie, an American archetype expressing both a universal aspiration for betterment and the meager resources often allocated to that goal. *Woodcut by Herbert Pullmeyer, Picture Collection, The New York Public Library.*

School Buildings Teach

The following section of *Civil Architecture* is about public school buildings, their design, and the educational programs they accommodate. Winston Churchill's comment that "we make the buildings which then make us," is particularly relevant to structures housing our youngest, most impressionable citizens. Schools are containers for teaching, learning and play; they also teach their own lessons through scale, materials, construction, organization, and architectural character.

Like human teachers, buildings can teach positive or negative lessons. Despite political exhortations to the contrary, forbidding, inaccessible, poorly organized, and badly maintained schools teach children (as well as their parents and teachers) that they are neither welcome nor important, and that no one cares whether they succeed or fail.

3.3. This view (circa 1840) of a teacher being stoned by students is a reminder that school violence has been with us for some time. *Picture Collection, The New York Public Library.*

Some positive attributes are seen as common to the schools presented here, suggesting design criteria appropriate for this most important building type. These criteria are organized below like a teacher's lesson plan, listed below the lesson they aspire to teach to the users of the school—pupils, teachers, parents, and staff.

This School Is For You, You Are Welcome Here

Schools should be welcoming and clearly express to children and their parents that their presence is enthusiastically desired. Entrances should be visible, usable and accessible. A convenient entrance for those with disabilities is no longer merely desirable and appropriate, it is now required by law. The computer term "user-friendly" comes to mind as a laudable design goal. The school building should make it easy to enter, find one's way around in, and use the available facilities.

The schools presented here invite with landscaped courtyards and entrance gateways, decorative fences, and mosaic murals. They welcome those who enter with a place to sit, art work on walls and ceilings, and a variety of spaces for before- and after-school activities.

Education Is Important, You Are Important

The challenge here is to balance sufficient monumentality to express the seriousness and significance attached by our society to education, with a smaller, more playful scale appropriate to children. A structure which is too imposing establishes the importance of the educational system at the expense of the individual, an overly child-sized scale slights the communal, adult aspects of the enterprise of education. Perhaps "modest monumentality" or "playful seriousness" express this sought-after compromise.

Civil-izers

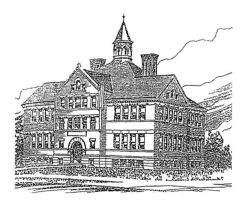

3.4. Late nineteenth-century public schools were sometimes somber and forbidding factories for learning. Illustration from Toward Better School Design *by William W. Caudill, F.W. Dodge Corporation.*

The schools illustrated on the following pages represent a range of size from a high school for 1800 students to a "mini-school" for 180 kindergarten and first-graders. The larger buildings soften their scale by breaking down into smaller, more comprehensible parts—classroom wings, sub-schools, gymnasium and auditorium wings. The smaller structures gain in importance by emphasizing roof lines, providing entrance gates, and recalling historical precedents, the "one-room" schoolhouses of memory and myth.

School Is A Very Special Place

This design criterion deals with the somewhat intangible qualities of "place," architectural "feeling," and "magic." We should not underestimate the effect of these factors. Nineteenth-century schools were sometimes seen as factories for learning, somber places of rigid discipline, rote learning and joylessness. The institutions immortalized by Charles Dickens' novels still have the power to strike terror in our hearts.

School buildings can help create a place which mirrors the more positive attributes of education—curiosity and exploration, whimsy and playfulness. The schools illustrated here have lighthouse towers, bell towers, and ceramic medallions picturing now-vanished former neighborhoods. They are laced (like shoes) with lines of colored bricks, decorated with brick rosettes, surrounded by artist-designed fences. Most of them are entered through (modestly) monumental gateways which express the passage from the everyday, outside world to a place of learning, magic and fun.

School Is A Part Of The City, Neighborhood, World, Universe

Having suggested that school is a special, *extraordinary* place, it is now suggested that the links between this environment and the larger world be emphasized. Beginning with the most familiar scale (nonetheless, a giant step for a young child leaving home for the first time), a school is part of a neighborhood, city, country, world and universe. The bumper-sticker admonition to "think globally, act locally" reminds us that we exist and act simultaneously in concentric spheres of influence and scale. Schools presented here are organized like city streets; illustrate the history of their communities; form part of a housing complex; enclose maps of the earth; and reflect the architecture of their neighborhoods.

This Is Your Home, You Are Safe Here

Security and peace have always been prerequisites for learning. A great deal of human energy has been invested in creating defended spaces, within which the time and safety needed to educate the next generation can exist. As ancient walled cities, medieval towns, universities, and monasteries are historic examples of this perennial human need, fences, closed-

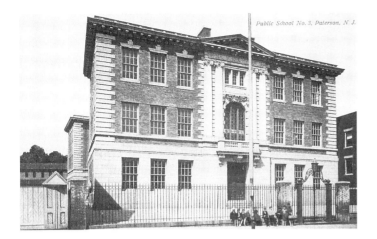

circuit television, intercoms and double locks are modern-day urban versions. In too many city neighborhoods, children confront a daily life as dangerous and frightening as any in history, without many of the compensatory supports of a traditional, cohesive culture.

Paralleling the need to protect is the requirement to provide a nurturing, "home-like" environment free of unnecessary distractions. Too blatant an attention to security concerns—fences, window grilles, even metal-detectors in some schools—can result in a school so forbidding as to seem not worth protecting. As in so many matters, balance and appropriateness are essential. The schools illustrated here are organized around enclosed, protected courtyards; have surrounding fences and gates unambiguously defining school territory; present "tough," protective exteriors, within which are contained kinder, gentler spaces appropriate for children.

School Is Part Of History

Each of us is part of a family, culture, religion, nation, and human community. Even the most creative individuals—those with the genius and energy to change the way we perceive and experience our lives—are rooted in a cultural and physical here and now. All buildings, but especially schools, need to reflect that continuity at the same time as they aspire to express a new perspective and possible direction for the future. As always, balance is everything. The illustrated schools which follow are conscious of the history of their communities and cities, as well as earlier prototypes of urban education.

3.7. P.S. 119 Manhattan represents Board of Education's chief architect C.B.J. Snyder's adaptation of a fifteenth-century French prototype to an urban public school. *New York City Board of Education Archives, Milbank Memorial Library, Teachers College, Columbia University.*

A visitor to Maxwell High School, on Pennsylvania Avenue in the East New York neighborhood of Brooklyn, would see a window into the New York of 1908, the year this school was occupied. The exterior form is a simple rectangle with extensions at both ends and at the center—approximating the shape of the letter "E". Large windows topped by gothic arches, patterned brick, decorative parapets, and a monumental entrance transform this somewhat basic form into a building of great dignity and presence.

Tall windows brighten the classrooms, and interior hallways receive natural light by way of clerestory windows from the classrooms and through Bauhaus-like glass partitions enclosing the stairs at either end. Although in need of renovation, the building is in surprisingly good condition considering 85 years of use by successive generations of children and teachers. A new coat of paint, updated mechanical systems and modern lighting will transform Maxwell into a cheerful place of learning ready for its next century.

The cellar yields two surprises. In one corner of the otherwise spotless boiler room is a bin filled with the coal that fuels the three cast-iron boilers (New York City has over 100 schools which are still fueled by coal). In an ironic example of the "law of unintended consequences," these schools are among the cleanest and most efficient in the school system, for the following reason: Coal is a "dirty" fuel, requiring careful handling and leaving a residue of ash after it is burned. The more careful the handling, the less cleaning required by the school custodian. The more efficient the burning, the less coal is burned, and less ash left to dispose of. The custodian's efforts to minimize ash result in very efficient schools.

The second surprise is the inscription cast into the fire-chamber doors of these boilers: *C.B.J. Snyder Architect New York City Board of Education*. This is an unusual but fitting place to immortalize the architect responsible for the largest program of American public school design and construction undertaken until recent times.

The tenure of C.B.J. Snyder as the chief architect for New York City schools (1891–1923) coincided with a period of massive immigration to New York City. (For an excellent brief history of school design in this era, see *New York 1900*, by Robert A.M. Stern, Gregory Gilmartin, and John

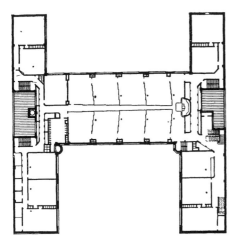

3.8. The "H" plan created two courtyards to maximize natural light and reduce street noise. Classrooms in the central wing were defined by movable partitions. *New York City Board of Education Archives, Milbank Memorial Library, Teachers College, Columbia University.*

Massengale, as well as Anne Rieselbach's "Building And Learning" chapter of *New Schools For New York*.) By 1898, 85 percent of the city's population was foreign or had foreign-born parents, leading the educational reformer Adele Marie Shaw to write, in 1902, of the city's "salvation dependent upon the conversion of a daily arriving cityful of Russians, Turks, Austro-Hungarians, Greeks, Arabs, into Good Americans." School buildings pre-dating 1890 were clearly inadequate to absorb this massive influx of students, and many of them were designed on the grim, Victorian model of factories for learning.

Superintendent of Schools C.B.J. Snyder was named head of a newly established architectural department of the Board of Education. He faced the difficult challenge of quickly building a large number of new schools in varied neighborhoods, and was committed to the most advanced theories of public education of that time. He needed a prototype for a school which would fit on most mid-block sites (corner sites were too expensive), provide natural light to each classroom, and create a protected play space. He reportedly found his prototype in 1896 on a trip to Paris "standing in front of the Hôtel Cluny . . ." This grand house, built in 1485–98, was organized around three sides of a walled courtyard.

3.9. P.S. 186 Manhattan (shown in this 1933 photo) is typical of Snyder's "H" plan prototype. *New York City Board of Education Archives, Milbank Memorial Library, Teachers College, Columbia University.*

In Snyder's version, two enclosed courtyards, placed back to back, resemble the letter "H", with each courtyard facing a different street. Classrooms ring these courtyards, with corridors along the window-less party walls. The center bar of the "H" houses classrooms defined by sliding walls, which can be stacked to provide an open space. This prototype would be repeated all over New York City, in a variety of architectural styles—Modern French, Dutch Colonial, and Collegiate Gothic. The standard features of the plan simplified the construction of many buildings in a relatively short period, while the variations in style, topography, and non-standard features (some courtyards had auditoriums built under them, etc.) gave each building a distinct identity.

Over the next few years Snyder combined the newly emerging technologies of steel frame construction and mechanical ventilation with architectural innovations such as large windows and sliding partitions to create schools (like Maxwell High School) which have served their purpose for almost a century.

Deja Vu All Over Again

3.10. Prototype Intermediate School 90, Manhattan, NYC: Richard Dattner Architect, 1994.

3.11. Prototype Primary School 5, Manhattan, NYC: Gruzen Samton Architects, 1993.

New York City faced in 1987 many of the same problems of immigration and school overcrowding it had confronted in 1887. The new immigrants were primarily Dominican, Haitian, Russian, Indian, Chinese. They joined their previously arrived brethren and other burgeoning communities in Washington Heights, East New York, and Elmhurst/Corona. New York continues its historic role as an engine of assimilation, responding to a world-wide increase in those seeking the American Dream at a time when that very dream is beleaguered and in question. Other cities, including Miami, Los Angeles, and Houston, face a similarly increased demand for school space.

Some factors have changed significantly since 1887, among them the size and complexity of government agencies, the demands for political participation by community residents, the size of the city itself, and the difficulty of acquiring school sites. In 1975, a severe recession almost bankrupted New York City. To save money, many older schools were closed, and a number of schools under construction were temporarily abandoned (only to be completed over the next several years at much higher costs). The procedures for planning, site acquisition, design, preparation of construction documents, securing approvals, and constructing a new school had become so complex, that the process could take from eight to 12 years.

A bold initiative was clearly needed, comparable to the effort of a hundred years earlier. A Mayoral Task Force studied and recommended a streamlined site acquisition process and a program of prototype schools. In 1988, the New York City School Construction Authority was created by the State Legislature to assume responsibility for building 50 new schools and rehabilitating hundreds more. Four architectural firms, including this author's, were each commissioned to each design three schools, utilizing a prototype plan which could be adapted to a variety of site conditions: Gruzen Samton Steinglass, and Perkins & Will, would design a primary school for 600 to 900 students; Ehrenkrantz and Eckstut would design a 1200-pupil primary school; and Richard Dattner Architects P.C. would design an intermediate school prototype for 1200 to 1800 pupils (a later version would add a 900-pupil version of this plan).

Universal vs. Particular

Prototypical, standardized designs of buildings have a long history in many cultures, particularly in military construction, where large numbers of men and material had to be housed, fed, and periodically moved to new locations. When Roman Legions established camps along the routes of their march, both the dwellings and the layout of these camps were standardized designs. During the two world wars, the armed forces in this country built thousands of two-story, wood-frame barracks of identical design, largely without special features reflecting their varied settings or climate. They were hot in the summer and cold in the winter, but they sprung up almost overnight to house the millions of soldiers mobilizing to serve their country. They also taught the important lesson that soldiers themselves were standard, hierarchical, and prototypical; of necessity, each had to be able to take the place of any other of comparable rank and skill.

Standardized buildings are best suited to serve universal, similar requirements. Often built in times of military or civil emergency, they offer the fastest way to accommodate the most people, usually at the lowest cost. They suffer from their sameness and inattention to local conditions. Architects tend to dislike standard plans; they obviously reduce the design work required and often leave limited scope for creativity and innovation. However, with the introduction of some flexibility and variation to take account of special conditions, they need not be as rigid as the military examples above. More benign standard plans like the carpenter's house plan books of the nineteenth century and the standardized, one-room schoolhouses of that time, allowed for a measure of adaptation of universal, ideal plans to reflect particular, local conditions and opportunities.

The prototype schools of the C.B.J. Snyder era were standardized plans which introduced variety primarily by varying their architectural style. Turrets, arches, spires, and the large number of stylistic features then available did a good job of concealing the repetitive nature of the basic plans. The fact that people were not as mobile then probably also helped to limit the number of similar structures a person could be expected to encounter. The automobile industry would soon be producing a similar standard product, with an increasing number of superficial variations (color, accessories, etc.) to introduce variety. Adequate at meeting universal requirements, standardized designs were developing possibilities of variation to meet particular needs.

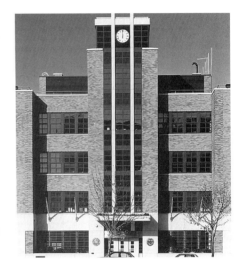

3.12. Prototype Primary School 23, Bronx, NYC: Perkins & Will Architects, 1993. *Photo © Chuck Choi.*

3.13. Prototype Primary School 7, Queens, NYC: Ehrenkrantz & Eckstut Architects, 1994. *Photo © Theo Coulumbe.*

3.14. Prototype Intermediate School I.S. 90, Manhattan, NYC, 1994: Neither historical nor overly modern, a traditional organization of base, middle and top helps these large buildings blend into most New York City neighborhoods. *Rendering: A.C. Bergmann.*

Two recent developments combine to make the "new" prototypes different from their predecessors: the computerization of the production of architectural construction drawings and the introduction of "modular" design. Computers in architecture allow for a design, once developed, to be easily repeated, varied, reversed, re-sized and re-combined to meet the special conditions of each project. Modular design entails the use of self-contained but interrelated components combined in varied ways to achieve a specific goal, much as a hi-fi system is assembled from interchangeable components.

Where the previous school prototypes primarily altered surface treatment to achieve variety, modular school prototypes designed with CADD (Computer Aided Design and Drafting) allow for wide variations in plan, number of stories, siting and elevation treatment by altering the combination of building components. Often characterized as a "kit-of-parts," this design approach clusters related spaces (classrooms, shops, gymnasium and auditorium, administrative offices) into components which can be "plugged together" in several arrangements. The four architects commissioned to design prototype schools for New York City each developed variations on this theme of combined, modular components.

Small Schools Within Large Schools

The intermediate school, a.k.a. middle school or junior high school, is a twentieth-century development attempting to provide a supportive environment for children in the transitional, adolescent years of 11 to 14, 5th or 6th to 8th grades. An appropriate building for this population should reflect their rapidly increasing maturity while avoiding the large scale and impersonality of many high schools. A balance is required between the more intimate world of early education and the independence and greater freedom of movement of high school.

There is a convincing body of research suggesting that smaller schools, particularly intermediate and high schools, benefit from limiting their

3.15. Prototype Intermediate School I.S. 2, Brooklyn, NYC, 1994: The central building section contains shared "downtown" functions—auditorium, cafeteria, library, gymnasium. Sub-schools are entered through protective gates and courtyards. *Rendering: A.C. Bergmann.*

population to between 400 and 600 students. The *Middle Schools Task Force Report*, published by the NYC Board of Education in 1988, recommended that "newly constructed middle schools be designed to house no more than 750 students." Advantages claimed for smaller schools include closer relationships with teachers and other students, better attendance and graduation rates, higher grades and test scores, and a more supportive environment at a time in our history when many children lack adequate support in their homes.

While the movement toward smaller schools has garnered growing support, several practical considerations weigh against this trend. These include the increased difficulty of obtaining the additional sites required (partly balanced by the greater availability of smaller sites), the greater cost per pupil of providing gymnasium, auditorium and lunch facilities serving smaller populations, and the increased time required to plan, design and construct two or three small schools in place of one larger building.

One increasingly accepted compromise is the creation of "schools within a school," where several smaller groups of students are administratively and physically organized as self-contained "sub-schools" within an existing building. The daily experience of each student is mostly within this group of 300–600 students, functioning with its own teachers, classrooms and administrators. The more specialized spaces—gymnasium, auditorium, cafeteria, shops—are shared, as are the mechanical services, staff locker rooms, and custodial services. Sub-schools can be organized around educational themes (business, performing or visual arts, music, science and technology, etc.) to focus a student's interest and provide an armature around which other required courses are introduced. The economies of scale of a larger facility combine with the benefits of more individualized instruction to make this an attractive option for both existing buildings and new schools.

3.16. A "kit-of-parts" of four modular
building sections can be combined in
several ways to fit almost any urban site.
Module A contains shared assembly, dining,
library, gymnasium and administrative spaces;
modules B, C, and D house classrooms.
Four-story prototype houses 1200 students
in two sub-schools, or 1800 students in
three sub-schools. Three-story version
houses 900 students in two sub-schools.

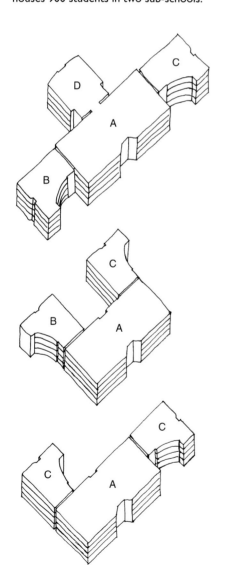

The program for this prototype was developed over a two-year planning
period involving Board of Education program specialists and staff architects, cost containment specialists from the New York City Office of Management and Budget, and the author's firm. Intermediate schools would be
built for populations of 1200 (two sub-schools of 550 pupils and a 100-
pupil special education component), and 1800 (three sub-schools of 550
plus 100 special education pupils).

After these two sizes were designed and in construction, a third, smaller
variation housing 900, consisting of two sub-schools of 450 children, was
developed. Like the prototypes of the 1890's, these schools would have to
fit a variety of sites, including the typically 200-foot blocks in Manhattan.

Uptown, Downtown

The prototype is designed as a community, with a "downtown" of shared
facilities and "uptown" neighborhoods of classrooms corresponding to the
sub-schools. The "downtown" module is a four-story, rectangular structure
containing administration, kitchen and cafeteria on the first floor, library
and shops on the second floor, and two-story-high gymnasium and auditorium spaces on the third through fourth floors. These shared facilities represent the communal activities reflecting the students' increasing freedom of
movement—they go downtown for public events (assemblies), sports events
(gym), eating out (cafeteria), manual work (shop), consulting archives
(library) and dealing with government (the school administration). A central,
monumental public entrance expresses the importance of education and
invites community use of these shared facilities during and after school.

Meanwhile, back at the "uptown," sub-school neighborhoods, the
mood is less formal, smaller scaled, and more supportive of the students'
needs for individualized learning. The 550-student, four-story classroom
modules are curved on one side to differentiate them from the rectangular
block, to enclose landscaped courtyards, and to provide a separate student
entrance through these courtyards for each sub-school. For the 1800-stu-
dent version, a third classroom wing housing 600 pupils is provided.

Lego Set Schools

With the "uptown" and "downtown" modules designed as self-contained
building units, all that is required for varying the arrangement of these modules is a "plug-in" connection, like *Lego* blocks. The "downtown" block has
five connection locations where "uptown" classroom wings can be attached.
With the computer's ease of duplicating or creating a mirror-image plan,
vertically or horizontally, over a dozen variations are available to fit almost
any site. Adding the variation in student population (900, 1200 or 1800 students) and the possibilities of varying surface color, texture and pattern,
allows each prototype not to replicate any other. A very old idea is new again.

3.17. I.S. 90 Manhattan—(top) the largest of the protoypes—uses three classroom modules to serve a total of 1800 students. A large site overlooking Highbridge Park allows for three student entrances and varied landscaped areas around the school.

3.18. I.S. 2 Brooklyn (middle) uses a linear layout to squeeze a 1200-student prototype into a long, narrow site. Play yards are at both ends of the site.

3.19. I.S. 5 Queens (bottom) is a 1200-student prototype with "uptown" classroom wings plugged into the back of the central "downtown" wing. This arrangement fits most mid-block sites with a plan resembling the original C. B. J. Snyder prototype. On this relatively large site there is ample space for outdoor play.

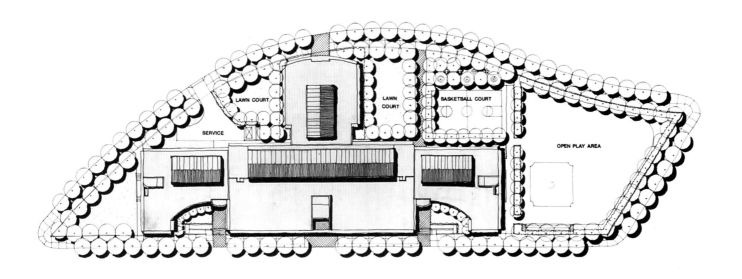

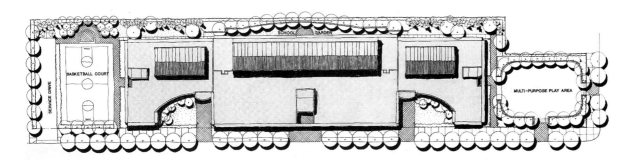

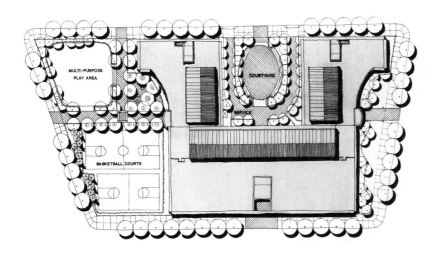

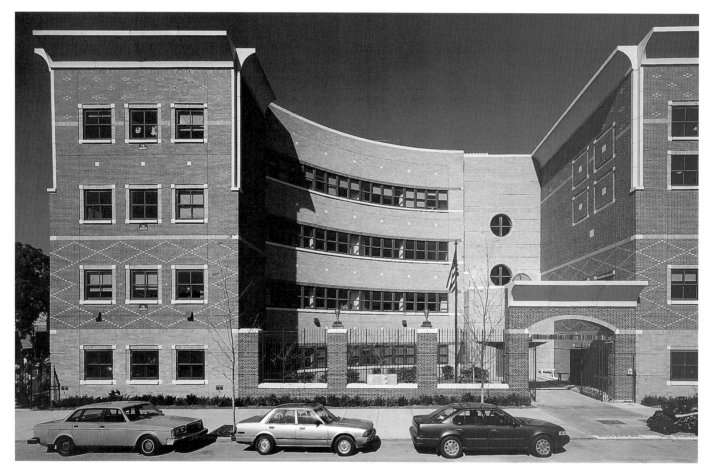

3.20. I.S. 2 Brooklyn. Crescent-shaped entrance courtyards of the sub-schools offer visual variety to the long street facade of this prototype. Brick colors vary for each site to harmonize with surrounding neighborhoods. *Photo © Roy Wright.*

3.21. I.S. 2 Brooklyn. Auditorium seating 500 is both the symbolic center of the school and a heavily used community resource for social, cultural and political events. *Photo © Roy Wright.*

3.22. I.S. 90 Manhattan. The community and visitor entrance expresses both civic significance and welcome. Shadow of the school bell is visible over the entrance. *Photo © Roy Wright*

3.24. I.S. 2 Brooklyn. Gateway designed by artist Ron Baron arches student entrances with a floating shelf of bronze books. *Photo © Roy Wright*

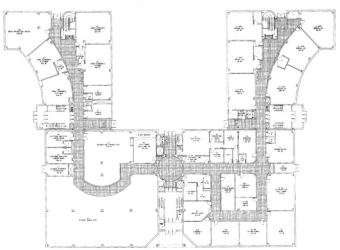

3.23. I.S. 5 Queens. One of four practical configurations for joining classroom modules to the "downtown" core.

3.26. I.S. 218's curved courtyard facade allows most classrooms to face across Broadway to historic Fort Tryon Park. *Photo © Norman McGrath.*

"The School of the Future"

3.25. I.S., Manhattan, 1993. A modern version of an urban school organized around an enclosed courtyard sheltered from the street. *Photo © Norman McGrath.*

When School Chancellor Joseph Fernandez and City Council Member Guillermo Linares (the first Dominican-American to be elected to that post in New York City) dedicated this new school in the Washington Heights neighborhood, they described Intermediate School I.S. 218 as "the school of the future." To Chancellor Fernandez, this project was "a dream of a lifetime coming true," the first of the "community schools" which constituted part of his ambitious agenda, and his favorite project. The community expressed respect for its heritage by naming the school after the Dominican educator Salome Ureña de Henriquez.

The "school of the future" designation reflects the fact that I.S. 218 goes far beyond the usual educational functions of a school serving 1800 sixth, seventh and eighth graders—it is also a health center, an after-school community center, and a satellite college for parents. This "new" idea has its precedent in the public schools, public baths, and educational alliances which existed in New York City during the vast immigration at the turn of the century. The innovation is in having three independent providing organizations sharing one building throughout the day, afternoon and evening, with the resulting efficiencies of building and operating one multi-purpose structure rather than three.

Bracketing the usual school periods are before-school and after-school activities operated by the Children's Aid Society, a voluntary agency which has been financing recreation, education and health programs for young people for over a century. Children can be seen by a doctor or dentist, get help with their homework, work on an art or crafts project, write for the school paper, or get additional practice at a computer. These extra-curricular activities are seamlessly integrated into the school day by simply adding periods to the normal school schedule—zero period, preceding first period in the morning, and periods nine and up after school. Nine hundred children take advantage of morning, afternoon, and weekend classes, making the most use of this well-equipped new facility, reinforcing their connection with learning, and offering an alternative to "hanging out" on the street.

The third institution sharing I.S. 218 is a satellite branch of Mercy College, offering adult education, remedial studies and college courses for credit. Parents (mostly mothers) dropping off their child can stay to improve their own education and employment potential—parent and child sharing, to their mutual benefit, the experience of school.

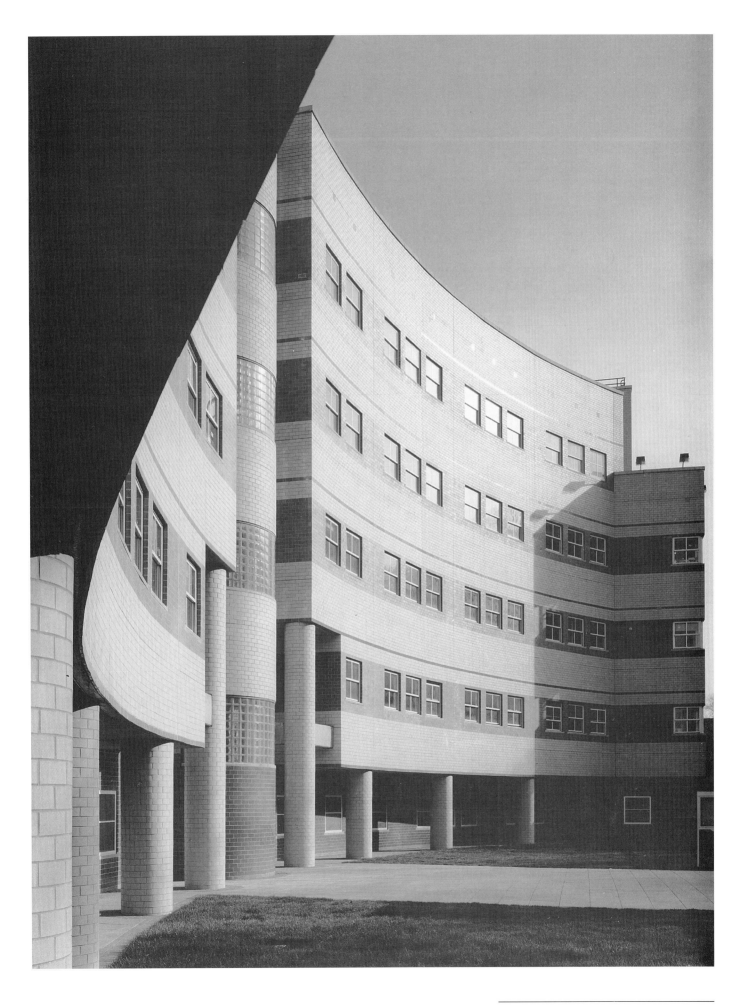

3.27. The curved courtyard facade welcomes visitors while respecting the scale and materials of the surrounding "art-deco" apartment buildings. *Photo © Norman McGrath.*

Classrooms are arrayed along the main curved corridor echoing the form of the courtyard, while special-purpose rooms, laboratories and core elements are located along the rear. A "rotunda" on each floor marks the center of the school, forms a transition with the angled auditorium and gymnasium wing, and creates a flexible, non-programmed meeting and exhibit space. The ceiling of this space is recessed to receive artwork, and a compass rose is set into the floor to remind those walking through the space that it is connected to the world outside.

3.28. The main student entrance is located at the "knuckle" between the classroom wing and the lower section housing the auditorium and gym. *Photo © Norman McGrath.*

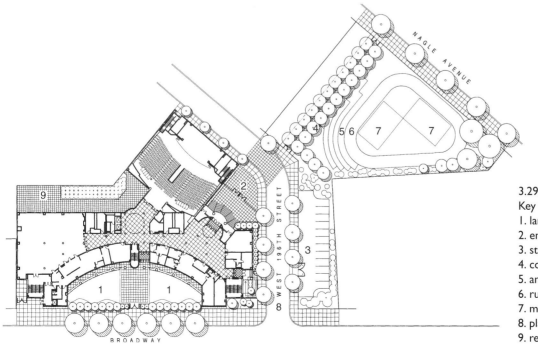

3.29. Site Plan:
Key
1. landscaped courtyard
2. entrance court
3. staff parking
4. connecting walk
5. amphitheater
6. running track
7. multi-purpose court
8. play street (during school hours)
9. rear yard

3.30. I.S. 218. The five-story school is a modest landmark in this Washington Heights neighborhood of six-story apartment buildings. *Photo © Norman McGrath.*

As previously noted, studies by New York's *Middle Schools Task Force* and other groups suggest that children at this pivotal age (sixth, seventh and eighth grades) need the personal attention and managable peer group that a limited population of about 600 students provides. Working against this laudable goal in this community were a number of factors—the difficulty of finding suitable school sites, the increased unit costs of building smaller facilities, and the difficulty of providing a suitable auditorium, lunchrooms and gymnasium in a smaller building. I.S. 218 is designed to take advantage of the efficiencies of a larger facility while allowing the student population to be divided into smaller social and educational groups.

The students are organized into four "academies" which stucture education around areas of related interests while sharing a core curriculum of language, communication and mathematical skills: an *Expressive Arts Academy*, which includes art education, music, and performance; a *Community Service Academy*, for activities related to the special needs of the neighborhood, working with the elderly, etc.; the *Business Academy*, which stresses job-related classes such as word-processing, computer skills, and office management; and the *Mathematics, Science, Technical Academy*, emphasizing robotics, math, science and shop-related learning.

3.31. Most students arrive at the school along this landscaped walkway bordering the playground. *Photo © Norman McGrath.*

3.32. A mosaic depicting Caribbean themes by artist Joyce Kozloff and monumental steps ennoble this student entrance. Handicapped access is provided by an adjoining ramp. *Photo © Norman McGrath.*

3.33. The school was named for the nineteenth-century Dominican educator Salome Ureña de Henriquez. *Photo © Norman McGrath.*

The design of the school building, like its tenancy, accommodates multiple goals. To create a welcoming presence for students and parents (for most of whom this structure will represent the most significant public facility they will encounter), I.S. 218 is organized around a large, crescent-shaped courtyard facing across Broadway to Fort Tryon Park. The courtyard also serves to distance the classrooms from traffic on Broadway while maximizing views of Fort Tryon Park. To reflect the importance of education for the future of parents and children, entrance gates mark both the courtyard entrance and the main student entrance on West 196th Street.

To respect the unique architectural context of this neighborhood of "art-deco" apartments, built between World War I and II following the completion of the subway system to this area, the school is limited to five stories. Bands of contrasting brick colors, glass block, curved stair towers, and decorative railings echo architectural features prevalent in the neighborhood, creating a sense of continuity with the past. The streamlined, curved surfaces of the building, and the landscaped courtyard have proved especially popular with the Dominican Community, recalling for many the buildings and gardens of their native country.

3.34. Rotundas on each floor will receive ceiling murals by artists selected under the Percent For Art program. The main floor rotunda compass rose helps orient the students to the world outside. *Photo © Norman McGrath.*

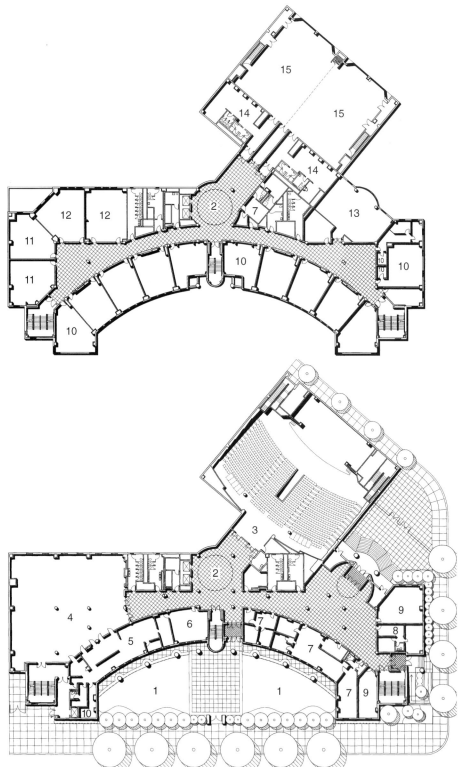

3.35. Floor Plans:
Key
  1. courtyard
  2. rotunda
  3. auditorium
  4. dining
  5. kitchen
  6. staff dining
  7. office
  8. medical suite
  9. community room
 10. classroom
 11. computer room
 12. word processing
 13. dance classroom
 14. lockers
 15. gymnasium

3.36. The popular dance classroom encourages rhythm, movement and balance.

3.37. Four well-equipped, networked classrooms facilitate computer literacy.

3.38. The auditorium seating 600 serves students, the resident branch of Mercy College, and important community functions. *Photo © Norman McGrath.*

3.39. A motorized movable partition divides this large gymnasium into two spaces for gym instruction. *Photo © Norman McGrath.*

Civil Extension

3.40. Maxwell High School, 1994. Rear elevation of the new addition. A curved stair tower brings this facade into harmony with a street of low residences.

In the low-lying flatlands of East New York, presently an especially dangerous neighborhood for African-American and Latino teen-agers, Maxwell High School's five-story bulk stands out like a cathedral in a medieval town. Like a cathedral, it is a sanctuary from its impoverished, unpredictable and often violent environs. Originally built as a prototypical elementary school in 1912, it was converted to a high school where overcrowding and inadequate facilities now require major rehabilitation and expansion.

The new 75,000-square-foot addition is an exercise in respect for the grandeur, scale and architectural character of the original. One story lower, to preserve the dominance of the main building, it continues the granite base, brick, and limestone string courses of the original facades, adding gently curved bays and curved roof profiles to further soften its impact.

The interior circulation of the addition extends the linear main corridor to a rotunda linking to the central corridor of the new structure. The main entrance of the older building is preserved as the community entrance leading directly to the restored auditorium. The addition houses cafeteria and kitchen, science laboratories, mechanical spaces serving the entire complex, and a student activity center. A large new gymnasium enclosed by an arched roof occupies most of the third and fourth floors.

3.41. Original materials, scale, and details are varied slightly in the new addition to both respect and update the 1912 original.

3.42. Architect's sketch shows the addition mediating between the scales of the original school and a historic Eastern Orthodox church on the facing corner.

3.43. The lower profile, curved facade and curved roof of the addition preserve the primacy of the original structure, which retains the main school entrance.

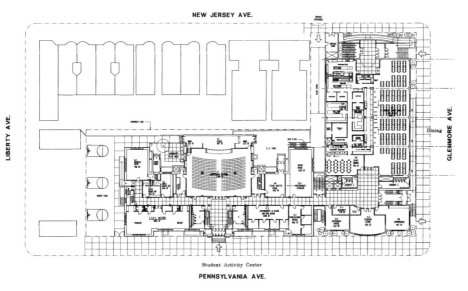

3.44. First Floor Plan: Axes of original and new buildings link at a rotunda in the addition.

A Little Civility

3.45. P.S. 11 Mini-School, Queens, 1992.
Overhanging roof with dormers and linear
skylight recalls Victorian-era schoolhouses
and improves the views of surrounding high-
rise apartment dwellers. *Photo © Rosana
Liebman.*

Rapid population growth among school-age children often outstrips a municipality's ability to identify, acquire and prepare new school sites. As overcrowding of existing schools grows more intense, community demands for school expansion often force a difficult option—the location of small school annexes on playgrounds adjoining existing schools. These classroom facilities (called "mini-schools" in New York) can range from portable classrooms to annexes whose 20-year life expectancy make them functionally permanent.

At P.S. 11 in Queens, a 300-pupil mini-school was joined to the existing "host" primary school by an enclosed corridor. The new two-story structure houses 12 classrooms for kindergarten and first-grade kids, who graduate to the larger building when entering second grade. This progression of scale from a small building for the earliest grades to the larger scale of later grades is one of the fortuitous consequences of the mini-school concept, along with readily available sites and the resulting ability to develop additional classrooms relatively quickly.

Construction costs approximate those of the more permanent larger new schools, as smaller buildings generally have higher per-square-foot costs. The major disadvantage is the loss of outdoor play space, so mini-schools are most appropriate for sites with school yards large enough to absorb this loss.

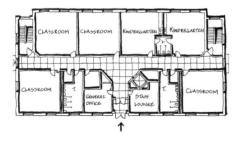

3.46. Second Floor Plan: P.S. 11 Mini-School
contains 12 classrooms for kindergarten and
first-grade kids on two floors.

3.47. First Floor Plan: P.S. 128 Mini-School encloses a play courtyard serving as entrance and buffer from the street.

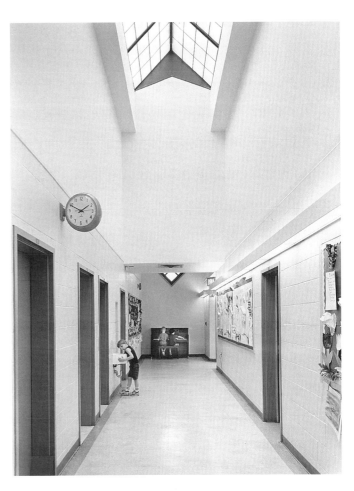

3.48. P.S. 128 Mini-School, Manhattan, 1992 (left). Entrance hall houses a building (administrative offices) within a building. Map of the earth is inscribed into floor tiles. *Photo © Rosana Liebman.*

3.49. P.S. 128 (right). Classroom corridors are tall and skylit to enliven interior spaces. Flags of countries these students come from (over 50 at recent count) are hung in this hall. *Photo © Rosana Liebman.*

3.50. P.S. 11 Mini-School (left) was sited along the street to leave enough space for outdoor play. *Photo © Rosana Liebman.*

Good Medicine

3.51. Pfizer School, 1993. Entrance hall of former Pfizer headquarters is now an appropriate school entrance.

Sometimes kids go to school in the unlikeliest places. Pfizer Inc., the pharmaceutical maker, has been located in Brooklyn for almost 100 years. As its physical plant grew, the administration center, completed in 1947 and still in fine shape, was no longer adequate and the functions it housed were moved to an adjoining site. Pfizer was looking for an opportunity to find an alternative use for their building. The NYC Board of Education, under Chancellor Joseph Fernandez, was seeking to locate school facilities in commercial structures to ease school overcrowding and to involve the private sector in this effort. And Beginning With Children, a foundation established by Carole and Joseph Reich, was looking for the opportunity to intervene positively in the lives of disadvantaged school children. The three groups found each other and a new alternative school was born.

The exterior of the Pfizer building already looked like a school. The interior proved suitable for classrooms, and the existing marble lobby was carefully preserved as the school entrance. New stairs and elevator rehabilitation were required to meet school requirements, and a small playground was developed in the rear yard. Private individuals, a leading corporation, a community, the Board of Education, and the School Construction Authority, successfully collaborated to produce a unique new school.

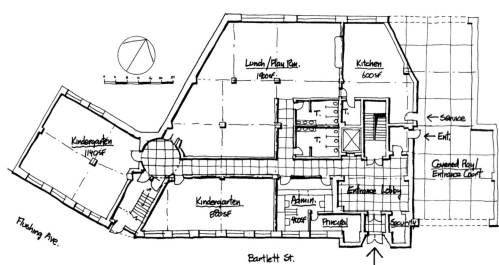

3.52. First Floor Plan: Kindergarten classrooms and future lunch/play room occupy this lowest level.

3.53. With a minimum of exterior restoration, this former corporate headquarters became an architecturally distinguished schoolhouse.

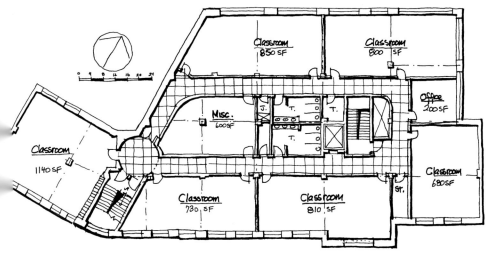

3.54. Typical Floor Plan: Exterior walls provide windowed classrooms while interior core is used for ancillary spaces.

School As Street

3.55. P.S. 380, Brooklyn, 1980. Boiler chimney, stair and elevator towers are expressed on building's exterior as a lesson in architecture and construction for pupils and community. *Photo © Laura Rosen.*

P.S. 380, designed in 1969 and completed in 1980, was an early attempt to bring some aspect of the outside world into the school. To make the facility easily comprehensible to children and their parents, a central corridor forms a "main street" from which tributary corridors serve the classrooms. (To the mostly newly arrived Latino families for whom this school represents a major contact with a civic building, this organization helps in creating accessibility and a sense of welcome.) This "main street" varies in width and accommodates small groups for informal learning situations. As in the life of a city, the in-between spaces are as important for social interaction as the programmed spaces.

The organization of the three triangular classroom wings along the linear spine allows all classroom windows to face landscaped courtyards rather than the street. The spaces available for after-hours community use—auditorium, gymnasium, large group room and early childhood classrooms—are on the first floor and may be used independently of the upper floors.

Flexibility Of Use

The program for this 1500-student, K-4 school provides flexibility for a variety of learning settings. Nine "learning complexes" provide self-contained areas which can function as either open classrooms for team teaching or can be partitioned into smaller, traditional classrooms. Ancillary spaces for each learning complex include a resource space, small rooms for individual instruction, a conference room, toilets, and storage. Additional flexibility is provided by the capability for extending the central spine and adding an additional classroom wing.

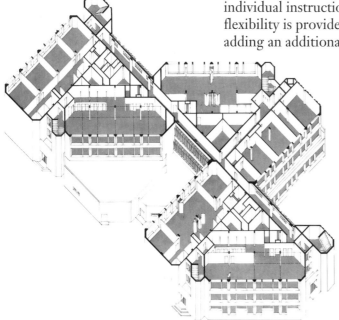

3.56. Picture window reveals the mysteries of the boiler room to potential engineers and architects.

3.57. Third Floor Plan: Central "main street" links three classroom wings in a simple organization instantly legible to students and parents.

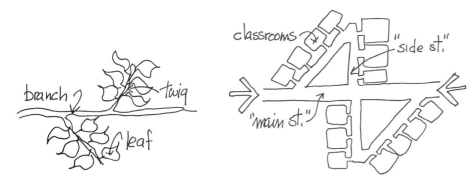

3.58. School's physical organization mimics nature's structure of branch, twig, and leaf.

School Buildings Teach

The school building itself was seen as a learning experience capable of revealing to kids its construction, utility systems, and operation. Air conditioning ducts and electric conduits are exposed in the ceilings of the "main street," and the concrete pan construction is visible in all learning spaces. The "main street" columns are color-coded consistently through all three floors, as are exposed pipes and ducts. When it rains, water collected on the auditorium roof forms a waterfall to the adjacent kitchen roof, and rain water flows though a glass pipe visible inside the school. A picture window allows children to look into the cellar boiler room. One of the first New York schools to be barrier-free, P.S. 380 ultimately became the Brooklyn Center for Children with Multiple Handicaps.

3.59. Outdoor spaces between classroom wings form protected play areas for children of different ages. *Photo © Laura Rosen.*

3.60. Rain water flows through a glass pipe visible inside the school.

3.61. "Main street," classroom wings, and stair towers are clearly visible from the street. The somewhat castle-like exterior houses a bright, colorful interior. *Photo © Laura Rosen.*

3.62. Artist Knox Martin has created a mosaic memorializing John Wayne, for whom the school is named. *Photo © Laura Rosen.*

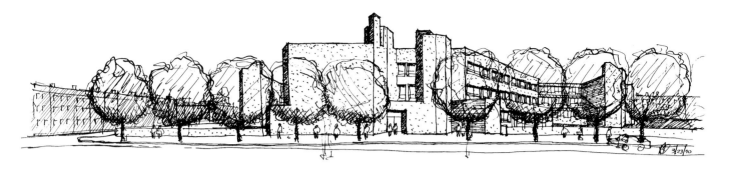

3.63. Early sketch of a classroom module "plugged into" main street corridor.

3.64. First-floor gymnasium is used by the community after school hours. *Photo © Laura Rosen.*

Public Schools Portfolio

P.S. 233, Queens, New York City: *Gran Sultan Architects*. One of the original mini-schools and specifically designed for retarded and disabled children, it attempts to normalize the students' experience and opportunities.

3.65. P.S. 233, Queens. Architectural forms are simple and easily comprehended by challenged children. *Photo © David Anderson.*

3.66. Natural light, exposed ducts and bright colors enliven circulation spaces and facilitate orientation. *Photo © David Anderson.*

E. Maria de Hostos Microsociety School, Yonkers, N.Y.: *Anderson La Rocca Anderson Architects*. "Real life" facilities—a marketplace, two banks, government spaces, media and publishing—help children learn about community life which is an integral part of the microsociety educational program.

3.67. Hostos Microsociety School. Freedom Square during market period. A physical manifestation of the concept of school as a microcosm of society helps convey the relevance of this special educational program. *Photo © Don Gormley.*

3.68. Stuyvesant High School. North facade expresses the 10-story academic wing (rear), seven-story physical education wing (left), five-story shop wing (right) and auditorium (center). *Photo © Jeff Goldberg/ESTO.*

Stuyvesant High School, New York City: *Cooper Robertson/Gruzen Samton Architects.* A "smart" building for smart students (Stuyvesant, Hunter, Bronx Science and Music & Art admit students by examination) at Battery Park in lower Manhattan. A tight site required a 10-story building with escalators. Interior finishes and equipment set a standard which should be emulated for every new school.

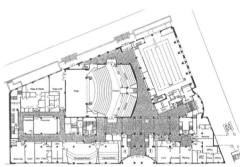

3.69. Ground Floor Plan: Functional components—classrooms, auditorium, pool, library—are articulated in plan and expressed in exterior elevations.

Wadleigh High School, New York City: *URS Consultants.* Opened in 1903 as a high school for girls, this C. B. J. Snyder "H" plan featured a 125-foot tower and large windows. The recent restoration creates a 500-student high school and three 180-student intermediate schools within the original building and adds a new gymnasium wing.

3.70. The new wing respects, but does not mimic, the architectural treatment of the restored original structure. *Photo © George A. Spence.*

Public Schools Portfolio

Perry Community Education Village, Perry, Ohio: *Perkins & Will/Burgess & Niple Ltd.* A vast education complex including three schools (K-4, 5-8, high school) each of which accommodates 1500 students as well as a community fitness center. Facilities are organized around formal courtyards and connected by an enclosed walkway.

3.71. The 850-seat high school theater is an important community resource; it is shared by the three schools and has television broadcasting capabilities. *Photo © Nick Merrick of Hedrich Blessing.*

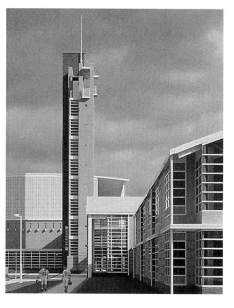

3.72. The architecture here creates a local landmark, a modernist version of Jefferson's "Academical Village," expressive of the vital function education plays in community life. *Photo © Nick Merrick of Hedrich Blessing.*

Capital High School, Santa Fe, N.M.: *Perkins & Will/Mimbres.* An 800-student school (expandable to 1300), where a mixture of architectural metaphors—rationalist, formal and contextual—are combined into a powerful civic monument. Its great power and simple dignity seem an appropriate response to the New Mexico desert landscape.

3.73. Colonnades unify the various building masses while providing welcome shade. Auditorium entrance is at the right, with the gymnasium wing visible beyond. *Photo © Nick Merrick of Hedrich Blessing.*

3.74. Stuccoed facades screen out direct sunlight while framing views of both building and landscape. This is a solution completely appropriate to its unique setting. *Photo © Nick Merrick of Hedrich Blessing.*

P.S. 234 Case Study

4

Whose Building Is This Anyway?
(Civil Property)

You buy a house, and the question of ownership is academic—this is your house. The architect of a public school—paid for by the tax dollars of countless households, regulated by Federal, state and local government, administered by a Board of Education, managed by a Community School District, watched by a PTA, staffed by administrators, teachers and custodians, and occupied by kids—faces a more subtle question: whose building is this anyway?

If you checked "all of the above," you were right. Here's a priority list based on professional experience and personal predilection: The kids come first. Their needs are foremost because they are most vulnerable, are undergoing the most rapid developmental changes, have the largest stake in the outcome of the enterprise. Next are the teachers, who spend their careers in school buildings and need to have their needs met so that they can best meet their responsibilities to the kids. After them come the administrators who direct and empower both teachers and kids, and the custodians who must heat, clean and maintain the school. Moving outward from the building, the other "owners" can be named: Board of Education, community residents, and government (local, state and Federal) like ever-widening ripples in a pond. And, last of all, the architect, the widest ripple, entrusted to contain and meet the needs of all the others.

When buildings have their dedication, the dignitaries, representatives, and officials come to make their presentations and have their pictures taken. And somewhere near the back of the crowd, among the kids with balloons, the architect stands after years of work, and gives away the building he or she alone will always own.

P.S. 234 Case Study

"In another city it might qualify as just one more well-designed school building, but in New York City, P.S. 234 stands out as a small miracle of humanity." (Ellen Posner, Learning Curve, *Architectural Record*, March 1989)

"All of us hear from friends all over the city who tell us how impressed they are by the school with the ship fence and the turrets . . . Visitors come from all over the world to admire and learn from this building—architects, teachers, college people, parents, elected officials. And our children, realizing the worth of our surroundings, take special care to maintain the beauty of the building." (Blossom Gelernter, Principal of P.S. 234)

"This project offers a model for public development projects. The process involved a broad range of participants from government agencies and the community in working toward a common goal. The process combined substantial participation with a realization that decisions had to be made to move the project along . . . there was a willingness to compromise on all sides so that the common goal could be achieved." (James Schmidt, Executive Vice President, New York City Economic Development Corp.)

4.1. P.S. 234, Manhattan, 1988. Turrets and rounded corners mark the borders of this Lower Manhattan school, recall the forms of older neighborhood buildings, and provide a community landmark. *Photo © Norman McGrath.*

The story of why and how P.S. 234 came to be is perhaps more significant than what was ultimately built. In a city where the realization of any innovative public project faces staggering obstacles, the school is as notable for what it did not do as what it did: it did not take the usual 12 years to complete; it did not disappoint its intended users; it was not forced on an unwilling community; it did not cost more than planned; it did not burden the operating agency with an inappropriate building costly to maintain and operate. It did represent a successful collaboration among city government, community and school representatives, the kids who would someday attend the new school, and the architect.

The Lower Manhattan neighborhood of Tribeca (**Tri**angle **be**low **Ca**nal Street) was the former "butter, cheese and eggs" district—the Washington Market—where masonry loft buildings housed New York's wholesale food distribution until the early twentieth century along what was then Hudson River frontage. The growth of the city's population forced the extension of Lower Manhattan into the Hudson River from its former edge at Greenwich Street on filled land. The construction of the World Financial Center on the most recent extension into the river at nearby Battery Park City, and the conversion of many loft buildings to apartments since the wholesale food market moved to Hunts Point in the Bronx after World War II, had led to a confrontation between commercial and residential proponents over the few remaining neighborhood sites. City government was trying to balance a desire to encourage large-scale

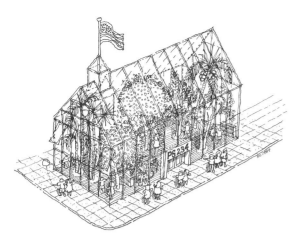

4.2. The earliest conceptual drawing by the architect in 1984 for the first site offered to the community, suggesting a microcosm of the outside world sheltered within a transparent, traditional schoolhouse.

commercial development to increase employment and the tax base with the increasingly vocal demands of a growing residential community which required public school facilities and opposed ". . . yet another monolith in the community."

The issue was joined when Shearson/American Express received a site designation from the NYC Public Development Corporation (now renamed the NYC Economic Development Corporation—EDC) for a large building to house "back-office" computer operations. Community residents opposed the project, seeking that site for the first new public school in the area to replace temporary school facilities (already designated P.S. 234) then leased on the ground floor of a high-rise residential development. A city-sponsored compromise was worked out where a portion of the Shearson site would be reserved for a small school. That site ultimately proved too small for both offices and school, and an alternative school site was selected which was large enough for a school and playground to accommodate the number of school-age children in the neighborhood.

4.3. P.S. 234 was ultimately built on a second, larger city-owned site within an area designated for high-rise commercial development. The building's shape and north facing courtyard aim at shielding its users from the scale and shadows of future development. *Photo © Jeff Goldberg/ESTO.*

4.4. One of the initial 1984 design schemes presented to the School Committee, which included a protective enclosure, north-facing courtyard, and a school bell at the corner of Greenwich and Chambers Streets.

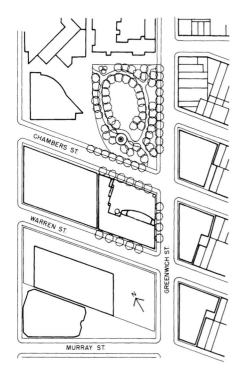

4.5. Site plan showing proposed high-rise commercial development south and west of the school, and the beautifully landscaped Washington Market Park to the north, across Chambers Street. These factors led to selecting a north-facing orientation for the school courtyard.

The unusual factors which would promote the success of the project were materializing. Two groups were now in place with a stake in the timely realization of a new school, EDC, which was willing to eliminate opposition to commercial development by providing a city-owned site and $14 million in construction funds, and a group of community residents and elected officials organized around the existing P.S. 234. There was now both site and funding, which in a typical public school project might involve three to six years of capital budgeting, site selection, community hearings, condemnation proceedings, and final site acquisition. Government commitment and an organized public constituency insured that government would be accountable for the success of the project, and that a vocal, politically knowledgeable community would maintain pressure for progress. The project now came into official existence, with a capital budget line and a Program of Requirements established by the Board of Education (BOE) which would now assume responsibility, under the watchful eyes of EDC and the community, for the construction and operation of P.S. 234.

Community Involvement

The community demanded, and was granted, a voice in the selection of the architect. The author's firm, and several others, were invited to make a presentation to a New School Committee consisting of local elected officials, neighborhood residents, the principal of the temporary P.S. 234, and parents of the children at that school. On the basis of prior experience designing schools and playgrounds, and a willingness to design the school with this group, the Committee made one of their first decisions—it selected the author's firm to design the new P.S. 234.

At the Committee's request, regularly scheduled, semi-weekly meetings were held over the next two years to discuss design concepts, review design proposals and monitor progress. The principal (Blossom Gelernter—a uniquely dedicated and sensitive individual of great wisdom and determination), teachers, parents and their kids would attend these meetings along with representatives of local officials and the EDC and BOE personnel responsible for project requirements and completion.

This meant that every two weeks the individuals who would fund, staff, operate, design and use the new school would meet together, a situation unique for the involved parties. It would have an extremely positive impact on the progress and outcome of the project for several reasons: the architect faced regular deadlines for presenting new design ideas to both funding agencies and the building's ultimate users; the government agencies were under similar pressure to expedite reviews normally taking months;

the school's teaching and administrative staff had the opportunity of influencing the design and relationship of program spaces, while learning first-hand about the space and budgetary constraints faced by the funding and operating agencies. Most importantly, disagreements between the various parties could be discussed and resolved on the spot, rather than generating memos which would solidify each contending party's position, consume valuable time and project momentum, and make compromise more difficult. (A similar approach, called "partnering," is finding growing acceptance among participants in building construction projects.) Some specific examples of decisions influenced by the Committee will illustrate the wide range of issues considered and satisfactorily resolved.

Issues Resolved

The earliest issues concerned the height, massing and location of the building on its site. Studies of the "footprint" for the projected 785-pupil, 75,000-square-foot building indicated that a one- or two-story building would not fit on the site. A four-story structure would fit, but would require excessive stair climbing for the K-5th grade population. The compromise was a three-story school (with basement) which would occupy about two-thirds of the site, leaving one-third for an outdoor play area.

One of the most difficult decisions affecting the final design involved the siting of this small building on a plot which would be surrounded by 10-story apartment buildings to the east, and far taller commercial structures to the south and west. To illustrate these conditions, the architect built a scaled massing model showing the bulk of all the existing and projected surrounding buildings. Moving a light source around this model to approximate the position of the sun in summer, winter, spring and fall revealed the shadows caused by adjacent buildings and allowed the Committee to evaluate with the design team the benefits and problems of various massing alternatives. A consensus was now reached which surprised all the participants. The selected conceptual scheme was organized around an open courtyard facing north.

Despite earlier assumptions by most participants that the courtyard should face south to take advantage of sunlight, the massing model demonstrated that the tall buildings to be built south and west of the new school would cast shadows over this space for much of the year. An additional problem with the south-facing scheme was that most classrooms would face directly on Chambers Street, the busiest, noisiest thoroughfare bordering the site. The north-facing courtyard scheme had several advantages over the other alternatives: the most sunlight on the courtyard; all classrooms faced either the courtyard or quieter Warren Street; the school

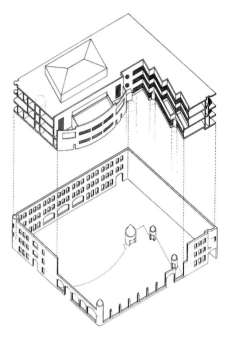

4.7. Axonometric diagram of the accepted "pearl in an oyster" design, with a "fortress" wall of traditional brick construction, corner lighthouse/bell tower, and decorative fence enclosing the school and play courtyard.

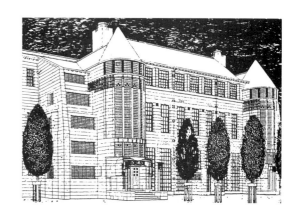

4.8. Entrance steps double as a small amphitheater, while the single, flowering tree introduces nature to this paved cloister.

and courtyard were oriented toward the beautifully landscaped Washington Market Park, visually pulling that open space into the new composition, and exploiting the slightly lower elevation of Chambers Street to give the impression that the Park and the courtyard were one space.

The varied requirements for the school courtyard were extensively discussed. It was to be the primary play space for four kindergartens, a playground for the older kids, an inviting community open space after school hours, and a refuge and buffer from the noise and traffic of Chambers and Greenwich Streets. This dialogue was expanded to consider the architectural character of the school. What was an appropriate expression for an urban school for young children in an historic neighborhood of a city beset by homelessness and vandalism? Out of questions like this, and the many design alternatives presented, came the organizing concept which would guide future designs. The school would be: a "kinder, gentler" environment, scaled for its students, within an enclosing, protective wall; a twentieth-century structure with horizontal, strip windows recalling the public architecture of the WPA-era sheltered within a contextual, fortress wall of brick turrets, gates, arches and rustication; a pearl in an oyster; a crusty, tough New Yorker with a heart of gold.

Design Precedents

Although this design concept may seem unfamiliar, it has many precedents in Europe as well as the United States. Glasgow's Scotland Street School, designed by Charles Rennie Mackintosh in 1903, and the prototypical "H" Plan School designed for New York City in 1898 by C. P. J. Snyder, chief architect of the Board of Education, share restricted, urban sites, and courtyards enclosed by strong, protective walls and gates. Other, older precursors of habitations sheltered within protective enclosures include the earliest known urban settlements, Mediterranean city dwellings, medieval towns and castles. Despite our understandable preoccupation with contemporary urban problems, we learn from a study of ancient buildings that the requirement of providing shelter and protection from hostile forces is as old as human history.

Much of what we know about past cultures has been gleaned from studying what remains of their built environment, and there are also examples of buildings which aim to educate their users. Cathedrals, mosques, pyramids and ancient shrines illustrated the iconography of their religions and the lives of their holy persons and deities in form, sculpture and text, especially before the mass availability of books, when most persons visiting those sacred precincts were illiterate.

4.9. Glasgow's Scotland Street School, designed by Charles Rennie Mackintosh in 1903, is still an appropriate prototype for an urban school. *Photo © Hamlyn Publishing Group.*

4.10. The entrance gate to the courtyard confirms that a special place is about to be entered. The community has access for after-school use and the gates are locked after dark. Three turrets guard the entrance to the school building. *Photo © Norman McGrath.*

4.11. Ceramic medallions by artist Donna Dennis depict scenes from the Washington Market which was formerly part of the surrounding neighborhood.

The architect suggested that the building itself, becoming an extension of the educational process taking placc in thc school, would teach its pupils and the neighborhood something about architectural history, construction techniques, mechanical systems, the history of both the city and the immediate community. Design, construction, history and learning would be woven into a skein of associations and references which both kids and adults could weave, at their own volition, into a tapestry of individual memory and meaning.

To illustrate the concrete realization of these design goals, here is a brief visit and guided tour, seen to the extent possible from the vantage point of a third- or fourth-grader (eye level about four feet off the ground).

The Surrounding City

From a distance of a few blocks, P.S. 234 looks much like one of the brick loft buildings in the neighborhood. Its red brick outer wall is punctuated by large, regularly spaced industrial windows; it is clearly a place where work takes place. From a little closer, one is not so sure. The turreted corners along Greenwich Street, the entrance gates into the enclosed courtyard, and the three turreted entrances in the courtyard, although playful and scaled to a child's size, have the protective mien of a fortress or castle keep. The main turret, at the corner of Chambers and Greenwich Streets, is more like a castle tower or a long-extinguished lighthouse. It is in fact both a lighthouse marking the former river's edge and tower guarding the small inhabitants of this protected place from the four- or sixteen-wheeled dragons which nearby exhale their fire and smoke. And, on every school morning, it is also a bell tower where a different child each day is chosen to pull a rope ringing a massive bell which can be heard for blocks, like a *muezzin* on a minaret, calling the faithful to learning.

From even closer, one sees that the wall and fence have been transformed by artist Donna Dennis into an open book, with inset porcelain medallions illustrating scenes from the vanished Washington Market, and silhouetted clippers, lighters, ferries, tugboats, and barges sailing perpetually along black iron waves. The building wall offers a lesson in traditional brickwork—curved brick arches, brick piers, brick rustication along the first floor, brick corbelling at the wall's top. From a kid's-eye view, you can't see into the courtyard until you enter through the main gate, leaving behind the traffic and the street, and entering the walled courtyard with checkered paving and a single tree, a cloister and magic garden. (Remember, you are in kindergarten or third grade and have not yet learned to forget the magic of a world of texture, color and wonder.) Once inside the gate, the fence of ships and waves makes cars and streets disappear; only a faint, quiet blur remains as a reminder of what has been left behind. In an

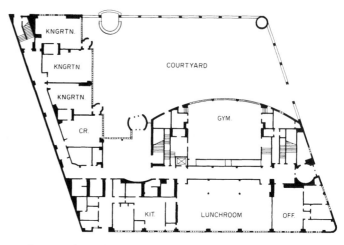

example of *synesthesia*, the overlap of senses, the fence and gate seem to diminish the sound by shutting out the noisy sight.

To an adult, the empty courtyard might seem like a pleasant but sparse place. It lacks the usual basketball hoops, playground equipment, and asphalt paving, seeming more like a European school courtyard than the usual American school playground. A single, flowering tree marking the main entrance and a hedge bordering the curved gymnasium wall are the two counterpoints to this hard-surfaced, outdoor room. Other design features include a continuous seating surface along the perimeter fence, and a checkerboard pattern of pink and gray concrete bordered by brick, with brick borders defining the path from entrance gate to main entrance turret. The somewhat minimalist design was purposeful, to discourage the appropriation of this play space by teen-agers and adults playing basketball, and to preserve the most possible free space. Devoid of people, it is an elegant but empty frame, a patterned rhomboid within a patterned fence.

A Backdrop For Kids

Just add kids, and the frame becomes a moving picture of ever-changing patterns, a Brownian movement of sometimes colliding particles, each atom with an individual purpose and plan. With a few props (balls, jumping ropes, Frisbees, toy trucks or dolls) or only with imagination, the grid becomes a fluid map of shared or individual meaning—paths, goals, boundaries, and turf define themselves by boisterous negotiation, or by a process known only to each map-maker. The maps overlap, as circles and lines of kids form, surround and penetrate adjoining groups, melt, and recombine into inchoate order. Around the edges, pupils and teachers sit on the enclosing bench to rest, think or decide which group to join. Like those racing around the patterned floor, they are at once participant and audience. The bells ring (a brass bell to mark the start of school, electric

4.13. The two smaller turrets provide for direct access from the first-floor kindergartens to the school courtyard. *Photo © Norman McGrath.*

4.14. With a few props, and their imagination, children transform this minimalist courtyard into an ever-changing setting for their play. Children on the surrounding bench can be both spectators and participants. *Photo © Norman McGrath.*

4.15. First Floor Plan: administrative offices, kitchen and lunch room, and four kindergartens with direct access to the courtyard. The gymnasium, requiring additional ceiling clearance, is four feet lower and served by a handicapped-accessible ramp.

4.16. The courtyard is paved in a checkerboard pattern and bordered by a child-sized bench. Each child can choose to join in one of many overlapping activities or watch from the sidelines.

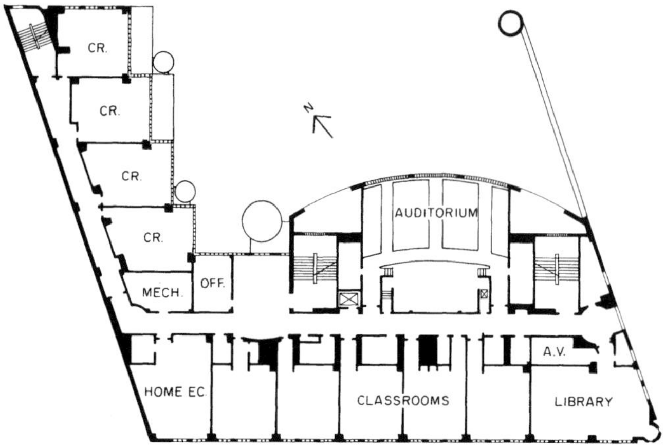

4.17. The lunchroom has folding tables and benches which can be moved aside when the space is used for rainy day activities. *Photo © Norman McGrath.*

bells to mark class periods) and all the maps dissolve, like an *Etch-A-Sketch* wiped clean, awaiting the next session.

Most children and parents arriving early spend some time in the courtyard before school starts. (In bad weather, pupils can play in the lunchroom until classes begin.) After the school day starts, the gates to the courtyard are closed and the space used exclusively by the school. After school, the gates are opened and the courtyard is available for community use until dark, when the gates are locked. An alternate school entrance on Greenwich Street is open throughout the day for visitors and late arrivals.

We have entered through the gate and gained the courtyard, but are not yet in the building; remaining is the third transition from street to school, three turrets guarding the entrance to the school. (To enter the fairy-tale castle, you always have to slay three dragons, correctly answer three questions, knock three times.) The two smaller turrets each serve two kindergartens on the ground floor, so that the youngest children can have the most direct access to the courtyard. The single, larger turret finally admits one to the school. The ceremony of arrival and departure, and the tripartite transitions marking both events, are there to make the experience *important*, and to reinforce the significance of what happens in the school.

Meeting Classroom Needs

The exterior design is site-specific, responding to the unique character of this site. The school's interior contains spaces that are less unique and more general, responding to pupils' and teachers' universal needs for classrooms which encourage learning, and appropriate spaces for assembly, play and lunch. The classroom (there are 24 in this school) is the most significant space in terms of the time kids and teachers spend there and the central importance of what should happen there. In the beloved one-room schoolhouses of American history and myth, the classroom was the only room. In modern schools the classroom still functions as home (homeroom), science lab, greenhouse, theater, place of rest.

Like its Victorian predecessor, the modern classroom should aim to be comfortable, well-lit and free from glare, cheerful and commodious. The earlier prototype is mentioned here because our informal investigations indicated that teachers, parents and children preferred those high-ceilinged rooms, with their tall, operable windows, to the classrooms in schools built after World War II. Unlike its forerunner, where usually obedient children faced the teacher in neat rows at fixed desks, with daylight streaming over their left shoulders, the contemporary classroom faces more varied requirements.

The modern classroom functions once more like the one-room school, with groups of varying sizes involved in joint or separate tasks, constantly reorganizing to accommodate a variety of activities. A group might be attending to a teacher at the chalkboard, while a smaller group works with a teacher's assistant or parent, several students work at the computer and others care for the class gerbil. Children are sitting at desks or tables, sprawling on the floor, typing at computer terminals, playing under a table, perching on the window sill, reading in a quiet corner behind a bookshelf. Like the courtyard, the classroom is a matrix for action, upon which are traced the myriad, intersecting patterns of the pupils' and teachers' daily tasks.

4.19. This kindergarten is like a one-room school, with groups of varying sizes involved in a variety of concurrent activities. Carpeting and cushions allow the floor to become a favored activity space. *Photo © Norman McGrath.*

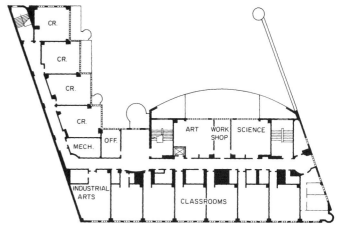

4.20. The "commons," with its stepped seating and oculus, has become a valuable setting for informal gatherings, performances, and study groups. *Photo © Norman McGrath.*

In order to accommodate this kids' *vivarium* (a place where living creatures are kept alive under conditions simulating their natural environment), the classroom is designed to take their special needs into account: it is a clean, well-lighted place, tall enough to let paper airplanes, and imaginations, soar; large, operable windows let in light, air (in good weather), and views of the surrounding world; energy efficient, glare-free lighting complements natural light, or replaces it on dark winter afternoons or evenings; acoustical panels absorb excess noise; easily cleaned vinyl floors ameliorate spills, while sections of carpet make the floor more inviting; perimeter radiation takes the chill off the large glass areas; air-conditioning allows for year-round use. Why shouldn't kids be treated as well as their gerbils?

The architecture lesson begun on the building's exterior is here continued by exposing the floor structure of slender concrete ribs made by pouring wet concrete over upside-down metal pans (pupils can replicate this process with pails of wet sand). The brick arches above the windows in the perimeter "old" wall are revealed inside the rooms so that children can make the connection between inside and outside. These arches can also be replicated by the students with blocks of wood or foam.

Lessons Of Necessity

The small-paned windows teach a different lesson, involving the interaction of physical and social factors. When New York City school windows larger than 30 inches square (30" x 30") are broken, the City's contract with school custodians (a document with significant impacts on the design and operation of school buildings) requires that outside contractors perform the required repairs, evidenced throughout the city by thousands of plywood covered windows awaiting replacement. Keeping each pane within this size limit, and keeping an "attic stock" of replacement panes, allows the custodian to immediately replace broken panes, avoiding the uncared-for appearance and invitation to vandalism communicated by broken windows.

The BOE and the NYC Office of Management and Budget require that school buildings be efficient (a net usable area to gross area ratio of 65 percent is mandated) and limit the gross total area (including stairs, columns, toilets, exterior walls, mechanical spaces) to 105 square feet per pupil for elementary schools. Every required space is listed in a detailed Program of Requirements which must be accepted by the Community School District before detailed design is allowed to begin, and there is little room for negotiation. The Committee and architect determined that each floor should have a space not on the program of requirements, a "commons" which could serve a variety of functions. Like the commons in a colonial village, this indoor open space would be shared by all and serve as grazing pasture (for kids), meeting place, and park.

4.22. The round turret windows are echoed in the oculus windows which provide pupils using the "commons" spaces on the second and third floors with a special view of the world outside. *Photo © Jeff Goldberg/ESTO.*

4.23. School corrridors provide lots of pin-up space for student projects and handiwork, reinforcing the idea that their own work is paramount. *Photo © Norman McGrath.*

P.S. 234 Case Study

4.26. Architect's sketch showing the planned treatment of the "commons"—painted constellations on the ceiling and a compass rose inset in flooring orient pupils to the world beyond.

4.24. The auditorium seats 220 persons in only 10 rows so everyone is close to the stage. As in all other facilities in the school, wheelchair accessibility is provided to the seating area and, by way of a back-stage lift, to the stage. *Photo © Norman McGrath.*

4.25. Decorative fence by Donna Dennis illustrates the marine history of this site, with silhouettes of clipper ships, lighters, tugboats, barges and scows. The stylized waves block views of surrounding traffic from a kid's-eye level.

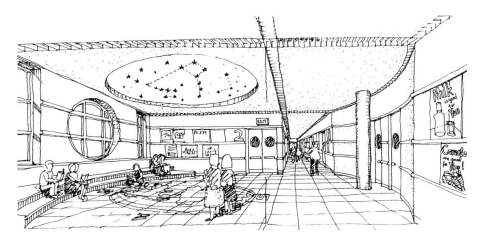

In order to provide this additional space, a few square feet had to be "borrowed" from the programmed space on each floor. (When BOE representatives complained that "stolen" would be the more appropriate characterization, the Committee responded that the small reduction in each room would not be noticeable or affect the spaces "borrowed" from, and would be "returned" in the commons.) The commons were built on all three floors, and have become intensively used spaces contributing to the successful operation of the school. On the ground floor, the commons is furnished with park benches, providing a welcoming place for parents dropping off their children to linger a while with their charges, with other parents, or with teachers. The message communicated by this space is that parents are welcome and are encouraged to participate in school and PTA activities. After the school day starts this commons is used by pupils and teachers as a gathering place for going out to, or returning from, the courtyard.

The commons on the second and third floors are somewhat similar. They also function as gathering spaces for groups of students going to or returning from somewhere outside the home room, but differ in several respects. Since they do not adjoin an entrance, they can function more as a plaza along a street. With their built-in stepped seating, cove ceiling, and round window (*oculus*, or eye) on the world, they function as the symbolic center of each floor. The artist for the exterior medallions and decorative fence was to have painted constellations in the ceiling recess, and designed an inlaid map of the western hemisphere for the floor, but funds ran out and these orienting features await additional funding.

At the suggestion of the Committee, the construction of P.S. 234 became an educational experience for the pupils (and their teachers and parents). The architect led tours of the construction site for small groups at various stages of the work to explain the excavation, driving of piles, pouring of the concrete frame, masonry, and finishing trades. Children took bricks and other building materials back to their classrooms, made their own constructions and wrote about their experiences. Teachers and parents continued their involvement in the process right up to completion by helping to select paint colors for the classrooms.

P.S. 234 was occupied by pupils and teachers in the fall of 1988, only four years after the project was started. The concepts of accountability and collaboration between affected parties became a model of sorts for new school projects when the New York City School Construction Authority assumed the responsibility for school buildings. P.S. 234 is still one of the most sought-after public elementary schools in the city, and remains to this date affectionately cared for, free of graffiti, and a community landmark.

4.27. P.S. 234 courtyard. A circle of children in a protected cloister.

4.28. The gymnasium is the one space requiring greater than normal ceiling clearance. It is dropped four feet below the surrounding first floor, accessible by stairs and a gentle ramp. *Photo © Norman McGrath.*

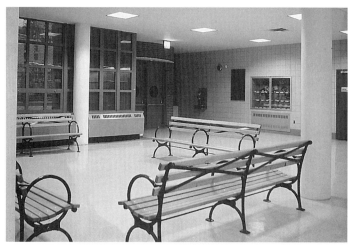

4.29. The first floor "commons" invites parents to spend time in school after dropping off their children, to get involved with school activities and meet other parents and teachers. *Photo © Norman McGrath.*

Public Education

5

We Don't Know Enough (Civil Ignorance)

When one has convinced oneself that our knowledge is boundless, it is corrective to consider the questions in Paul Gauguin's painting titled: "Who are we? Where do we come from? Where are we going?" What about some simpler questions that one would expect an architect to be able to answer: What proportions make a space inviting? Does the color of a building affect passersby? What is the effect of a high-rise building on the micro-climate of the surrounding neighborhood? What is the human cost of working for eight hours in a windowless room under fluorescent lights?

The effects of buildings on their occupants, visitors and neighbors are more poorly understood now than they were in antiquity. Vitruvius's "commodity, firmness and delight" were adequate measures of architectural intention and performance in their day, but need augmenting to deal with present buildings of immense scale and mechanical complexity. The lack of an objective measure of the effect of our built environment on our lives and well-being is especially surprising in this scientific age. We can measure air quality (lack of quality, or pollution, is what we actually measure), lighting levels and temperature, but there is no accepted measure for the psychic comfort, freedom from distraction or productivity enhancement of a building or space. There is much left to learn. And know.

5   Public Education

A Lifetime of Learning

5.1. Townsend Harris Hall at the City College/CUNY of New York. For many decades, more graduates of this public college attained doctoral degrees than those of any other institution. In this learning laboratory, 1905 meets 1995. *Photo © Rosanna Liebman.*

Along with public schools, public universities and public libraries were once the primary institutions of education for newly arrived immigrants, their children, and others of limited means but unlimited aspirations. These places of learning still serve that essential role in the life of new generations seeking political freedom and the opportunity for economic advancement. Despite daily media reports enumerating the shortcomings of public education, such facilities continue to impart learning and civility to hundreds of thousands every year.

A visitor to the Flushing Branch Library in Queens, New York City, would see hundreds of adults and children (Russian, Chinese, Korean, Haitian, and a dozen other ethnic groups) sitting and standing in every available spot, absorbed in newspapers, magazines and books. A guest at graduation ceremonies at one of New York City's special high schools could hear a valedictory address of great beauty and intelligence from someone who had arrived in this country four years before without the slightest understanding of English. Although burdened by inadequate funding and insufficient public support and appreciation, for those prepared to take advantage of these offerings, these civic institutions continue to work.

Changes in the global economy make all of us, professionals and factory workers alike, recent immigrants to a world requiring the constant mastery of new skills and education in multiple new languages. In this evolving milieu, the distinctions between child and adult, native-born or foreigner, are increasingly irrelevant. All over the world, patterns of seniority, company loyalty to employees (and the reverse), and guarantees of employment are being supplanted by much more fluid and impermanent associations of organizations and individuals based on skill, economic advantage and convenience. While this may be good for productivity on a global scale, it will require a lifetime of learning and hard work for the individual.

Several recent administrations have made much of America's need to become more competitive internationally by becoming more productive domestically. The education and re-education of our entire population is often mentioned as a civic goal of primary importance. If this essential goal is to be achieved, the constellation of civic institutions of learning on which most of us depend will have to be nurtured and greatly expanded.

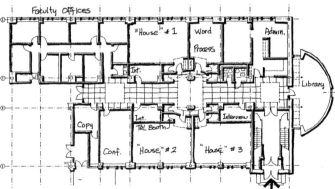

5.2. CUNY Law School Legal Clinic: Real world clients bring legal problems to law school students working under the supervision of faculty in a setting approximating the office of a private law firm.

5.3. CUNY Law School Legal Clinic Floor Plan: Corridor nodes outside four group study rooms become settings for informal meetings.

First, Do No Harm

5.4. The collegiate gothic campus of City College was designed in 1905 by George Post. Townsend Harris Hall was restored and reconfigured to house the School of Nursing and learning centers for English and mathematics. *Photo © Rosanna Liebman.*

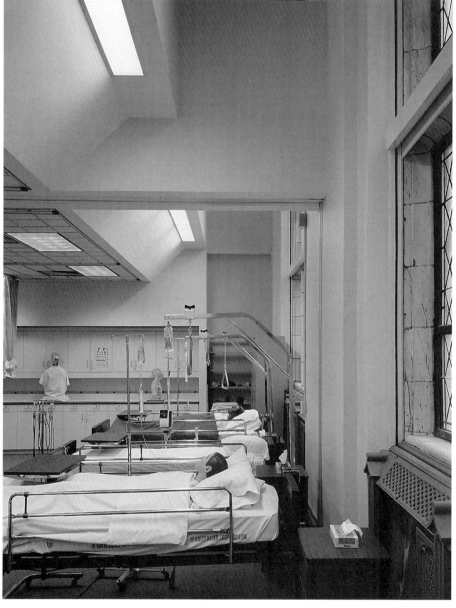

5.5. Nursing students train in a realistic hospital ward inserted into the former auditorium of this historic landmark. New construction is kept away from exterior walls to preserve the large gothic windows. *Photo © Rosanna Liebman.*

5.6. Section showing the new intermediate floor constructed within the original auditorium volume. Nursing School offices occupy the new level over the teaching wards.

5.7. Windows of the new administrative office floor are set back from the gothic fenestration, bringing natural light into both offices and wards below. *Photo © Rosanna Liebman.*

5.8. Separating new construction from the historic building skin allows the new spaces to have a contemporary design without compromising the original. Circulation spaces are restored to the original 1905 design. *Photo © Rosanna Liebman.*

Collegiate Civility

5.9. Central corridor of Boylan Hall, renamed Boylan Boulevard to reflect its new role as student "main street," organizes the areas along it—servery, dining spaces, all-night diner. This design reflects the "streamlined modern" interiors of other campus buildings.

The flowering of public architecture during the WPA gave Brooklyn, in 1937, a public college which expressed the duality of that time of contradictions. Georgian brick exteriors dignify campus buildings around a landscaped quadrangle rivaling the Ivy League, while long, tile-faced interior corridors with fluorescent lighting express a stripped-down "Streamlined Modern" esthetic of limited means and practical materials. True to the duality at its inception, Brooklyn College continues to offer a Harvard experience to riders of the subway's "D" train. Its student population likewise veers from Haitians to Hasidim, Russians to Rastafarians, teen-agers to senior citizens.

On warm, sunny days, the main quad is the heart and soul of the College; for all the other times, an indoor center was badly needed. The new dining facility for students, faculty and staff in the basement level of Boylan Hall was designed to create such a center.

5.10. Architect's sketch shows the faculty dining room as an exhibit space for paintings by faculty and students.

5.11. Reflecting the traditional design of the 1937 campus, table service for faculty and students is available under the nine vaulted skylights of the Georgian Room.

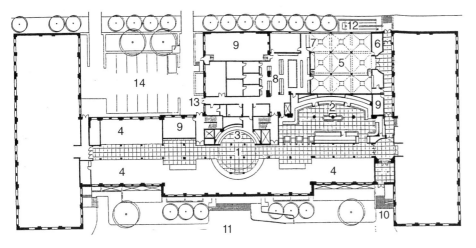

5.12. Floor Plan:
Key:
1. student cafeteria
2. servery
3. dairy bar
4. seating areas
5. Georgian Room
6. private dining room
7. wine bar
8. kitchen
9. mechanical
10. entrance from quad
11. quadrangle
12. access ramp
13. service entry
14. parking, service

Modest Monumentality

5.13. Through this (modestly) monumental gate pass adults and children seeking wisdom, fun and a good read. The gate emphasizes the civic importance of this building, and the fan-shaped grille echoes the shape of the entrance courtyard. *Photo © Laura Rosen.*

The program for this 7500-square-foot branch of the New York Public Library called for a modest building with several design restrictions: a single floor (for handicapped accessibility and supervision); no structure higher than 14 feet (for budgetary reasons); no windows on the street line or skylights (due to security and possible vandalism). The site presented additional problems—it faced a busy commercial street with an elevated subway. Within these strict conditions, the challenge was to create a building expressing the civic importance of this long-awaited library to a community with large numbers of elderly readers and young children new to books and learning.

In an example of "architectural triage" (see p. 41), the limited resources available are concentrated on one bold design gesture—a crescent-shaped entrance courtyard. This form resolves several design goals: creating an appropriately important transition space between street and library; creating a safe reading and play space for children; allowing for a continuous, curved band of south-facing windows pulled back from the noisy street; and protecting the library precincts by a decorative fence. Library readers have daylight to read by, and passersby can look into the library and be enticed, perhaps, to use it.

5.14. The children's library and reading room (seen here) faces the courtyard and is visible from the central check-out station. Beyond are library offices, work rooms, storage and rest rooms. *Photo © Laura Rosen.*

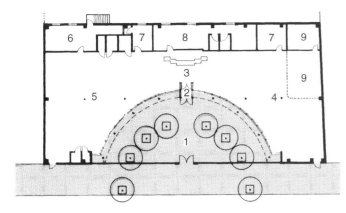

5.15. Floor Plan:
Key:
1. courtyard
2. entry
3. control
4. children's reading room
5. adult reading room
6. mechanical
7. librarian
8. workroom
9. meeting room

5.16. Courtyard both protects the library from street noise and traffic and welcomes library users. A special welcome is extended to kids by artist Marcia Dalby's fiberglass kangaroo, dinosaur and frog. *Photo © Laura Rosen.*

Public Education Portfolio

Student Housing and Dining Facility, University of Virginia: *Tod Williams Billie Tsien Architects.* The architects comment: "These buildings attempt in a modest way to inscribe a new set of boundaries and spaces for the University of Virginia . . . As Jefferson's original site plan framed an open horizon, The New College looks out to the Blue Ridge Mountains, and shares with Jefferson's vision the desire to create a place with a strong sense of both center and edge." A fine example of a modernist intervention respecting a classical landmark.

5.17. Principal's house at the top of the hill, and dormitories marching down the hill, frame a view of the dining facility and student center as well as the Blue Ridge Mountains beyond. *Photo © Michael Moran.*

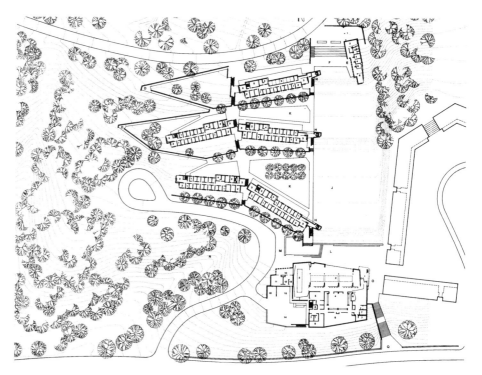

5.18. Site Plan: What might appear random in plan makes perfect sense in its three-dimensional relation to site and landscape.

Bellevue Regional Library, Bellevue, Washington: *Zimmer Gunsul Frasca Partnership Architects.* Balancing an exterior civic monumentality with more intimate interior spaces, mediating between downtown development on one side and a residential neighborhood on the other, serving as both information hub and community center, this library exemplifies and successfully resolves the complex requirements of civic architecture.

5.19. Bellevue Library (above). The sheltering metal shed roofs use an agricultural vernacular to unify, shade, and protect the building's elevations. An overhanging "porch" (at right) defines the main library entrance. *Photo © Timothy Hursley.*

5.20. Stack and reading areas are filled with natural light and busy readers demonstrating the community's affection for this civic amenity. *Photo © Timothy Hursley.*

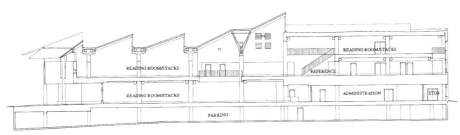

5.21. Section: Monitor roofs fill the reading rooms with natural light; parking is largely below grade to preserve the site.

Public Education Portfolio

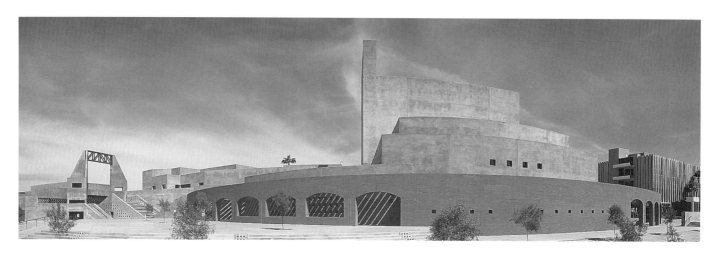

Arizona State University Fine Arts Center, Tempe, Arizona: *Antoine Predock Architect.* This civic center for the arts derives its power from an assemblage of pueblo-like forms under a desert sky. One experiences the building as a theatrical narrative whose meaning remains tantalizingly obscure.

5.22. The sweeping arc of the red brick arcade/aqueduct provides a shaded, processional walkway leading circuitously (turn right at the fountain) to the theater lobby. *Photo © Timothy Hursley.*

5.23. The junction between performance spaces (right) and museum spaces (left) is a civic assemblage reminiscent of Anasazi cave dwellings. A cubist collage breaks down this huge structure into components of human scale. *Photo © Timothy Hursley.*

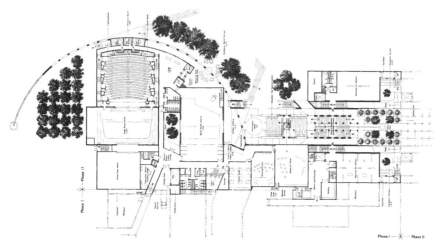

5.24. First Floor Plan.

University of Nebraska Fine Arts Building, Omaha, Nebraska: *Hardy Holzman Pfeiffer Associates/The Schemmer Associates, Architects*. The major building component is a four-story masonry wing whose undulations recall nearby grain silos. Two galleries for changing exhibitions and a 200-seat theater frame both ends of the structure. Civic scale is achieved through bold, simple forms and rich, simple materials.

5.25. Fine Arts Building and grain silo in the distance rise dramatically from the Nebraska prairie like cathedrals in the French countryside. *Photo © Thomas Kessler.*

5.26. Gently undulating facades (like Jefferson's garden wall at the University of Virginia) soften the 300-foot length of the main facade. *Photo © Thomas Kessler.*

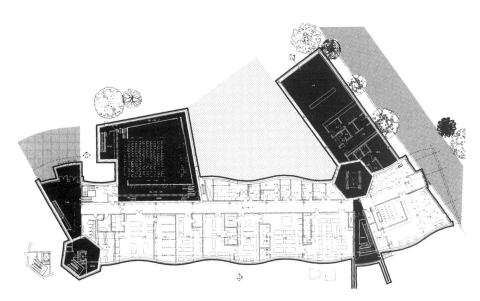

5.27. Main Floor Plan: Special spaces (theater and exhibit galleries) punctuate the undulating, linear wing of teaching and administrative spaces. *Photo © Thomas Kessler.*

Public Education Portfolio

Bucks County Free Library, Doylestown, Pennsylvania: *Bohlin Cywinski Jackson Architects.* Civic presence is here established by ennobling the forms of nearby rural buildings and increasing their scale to respond to the adjoining historic prison and Mercer County Museum.

5.28. Monumental circulation spine extends to the street, defining the library entrance and matching the scale of neighboring structures. *Photo © Christopher Barone.*

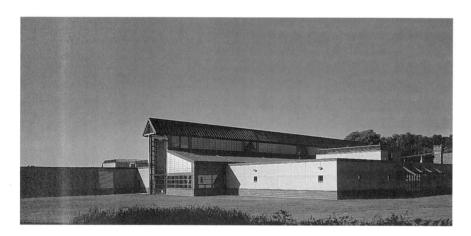

5.29. A vernacular simplicity here becomes civic grandeur. *Photo © Christopher Barone.*

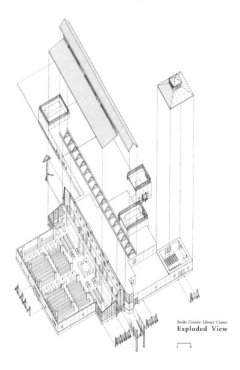

Bucks County Library Center
Exploded View

5.30. Circulation spine runs the length of the library, organizing reading rooms, stack areas, and ancillary spaces in a form instantly legible to visitors.

Public Works

The Second Law of Thermodynamics

It was said by C. P. Snow that not knowing the Second Law of Thermodynamics was comparable to never having read a work by Shakespeare. This fundamental principle describes the transformation of energy and the asymmetry intrinsic to nature: hot objects cool, but not the reverse; bouncing balls come to rest, clocks wind down, water falls, things break, fire consumes wood, gases disperse—but not the reverse.

The Second Law is about corruption and decay, the slippery slope leading from order to chaos. For any natural change entropy increases, and the universe tends to a final, featureless inertness, where everything has come to rest at the same temperature. The energy, heat and order of the universe are finite and diminishing. We borrow that energy from our sun (as wind, heat, plants, animals, coal, oil) to create wonderfully intricate islands of temporary order and life among the relentless dissolution. The lessons of this oddly liberating science for architects (and others) include these two:

***Waste Not, Want Not!** Use the transient physical gifts of our shrinking world well. Even renewable resources are not so forever, the non-renewable vanish at an alarming and increasing rate. Build efficiently and well, to last a long time. Consider the human and physical energy affected by your design decisions: siting, building form, selection of materials, mechanical systems.*

***Seize The Day!** Architects and engineers are entrusted by society with the responsibility of ordering the built world. Each creation of order from the surrounding chaos is a noble, civic undertaking. Making a school, a bridge, a blast furnace, or a circle of stones, is both a necessary and heroic act of communal faith in the face of chaos. Depending on your belief, it can affirm either God or Man.*

It almost reverses, for a while, the irreversibility of time.

6   Public Works

6.1. Marine Transfer Station, West 59th St. The dignity of all human endeavor can find appropriate expression even in the design of solid waste treatment facilities.

6.2. Marine Transfer Station, West 59th St. The Vitruvian injunction for architecture to achieve "firmness, commodity, and delight" holds equally true for civic infrastructure.

We're All Connected

This advertising tag line and jingle for New York Telephone expressed both the social interrelatedness of modern civilization and the telephone wires linking us together. Also coming into our homes are wires carrying electricity, water pipes, gas pipes, and television cables. Leading from our homes are sewage pipes, bags of garbage, and recyclable materials. Less physically tangible connections are: the air we consume and exhaust in breathing and combustion; the electronic waves carrying radio, television and, increasingly, communication; and deliveries of mail and packages.

The present electronic revolution (fiber optic cables, wireless communication, the merging of electronic systems now possible) is breaking down the distinction between what is coming *in* to our dwellings and what is going *out*. In addition to the familiar two-way phone, electric and gas meters can now be read remotely, television is becoming interactive, even electric wires can carry communication channels. We are all connected more than ever before.

These expanding electronic and wireless connections are changing our world by expanding our choices (and multiplying our diversions), allowing us to work from home (and increasing our isolation), raising our productivity (and making more of us redundant), enhancing our personal effectiveness (and diminishing our public environment).

The physical manifestations of our interrelatedness—the reservoirs, water purification plants, refuse collection and recycling facilities, sewage plants, sludge processing structures, composting facilities—are also changing in response to technical progress, increasing population, community concern and opposition, and a better understanding of the consequences of pollution. The architectural design of the vast facilities required to meet this growing, world-wide need is an essential component of integrating these buildings into communities, expressing the heroic scale of this communal undertaking, and providing cost-effective, long-lasting structures.

There's A Small Hotel

Twenty years ago, while staying in a small hotel on the shore of a pristine and spectacularly beautiful Scottish lake appropriately named *Loch Awe*, I was surprised to see the hotel's garbage loaded into a small rowboat, rowed to the middle of the lake, and dumped into the clear water. The rowers were equally surprised by my protests to their action—this was the way they had always disposed of their garbage. They patiently explained to me that few people lived along the shores of this vast lake, the lake was very deep, and the amount of garbage was far too small to have any effect on the water. I wasn't totally convinced but deferred to their local wisdom and long tradition. It was, after all, their lake.

About 10 years later, on a subsequent visit, many more houses could be seen along the lake shore. The hotel's garbage was no longer sent to the bottom of the lake, it was collected and taken to a landfill disposal site. Whether the lake had begun to show the effects of generations of accreting refuse, or increasing ecological sensitivity had changed the hotel's policy, the myth of an easy balance between man's production of waste and nature's ability to absorb it was irretrievably lost.

In a sparsely populated country of abundant natural resources, man's use of resources and the waste products of that use could be largely ignored. Depleted resources and accreted wastes alike could be abandoned for greener pastures. Native Indians and Eskimos didn't so much live in perfect balance with the land and water (like us, they created waste, depleted local resources, over-populated fragile ecosystems), as live within the limits of their larger environment to absorb the depletion and waste created by their relatively small populations.

6.3. Portsonachan, on the shore of Loch Awe, Scotland, abandoned the temporary illusion of dumping its waste into this pristine lake at no cost to its purity.

6.4. Marine Transfer Station, West 59th St. If we are what we eat, are we not also what we throw away? *Photo © Stanley Greenberg.*

6.5. Fuller dome, World's Fair, Montreal. Buckminster Fuller was a prophet of seeing our environment as "spaceship earth" where all living beings are linked in a physical setting of matter and energy requiring conservation and an economy of means.

6.6. The town "dump" at East Hampton is a shopping center in reverse, a dropping center for the detritus of daily life.

In a world of 5.4 billion people, growing at the rate of 100 million people (the total population of Central America) per year, dealing with waste—human, solid, liquid, gaseous, radioactive, contaminated—has become an issue central to our survival. The economy, simplicity and luxury of dumping our leavings into the nearest lake is no longer possible. Where traditional societies could rely on earth, water, fire and air for their waste disposal, modern man is a passenger on what R. Buckminster Fuller prophetically named "spaceship earth." Like our astronauts, we travel in a vulnerable vessel, with limited resources and the necessity of controlling, recycling and living with our waste.

Fuller (1895–1983) was an inventor, architect, educator, philosopher and visionary whose major contributions were largely ignored by the increasingly affluent and consumer-oriented post-World War II society. Recognized initially for designing the futuristic and commercially unsuccessful Dymaxion House in 1927 and Dymaxion Car in 1934, Fuller went on to develop the Geodesic Dome structures first commercially constructed in 1952 and ultimately built around the world. Among his lasting contributions are his recognition of the interrelatedness of man and environment and his passionately held belief of the necessity of conserving resources and minimizing waste, in his words, to derive "maximum gain of advantage from minimal energy input." The architecture of public facilities in a time of economic dislocation and limited resources has a special responsibility to attend to this maxim.

Shop Till You Drop

The former town dump is now called a disposal and recycling center and is a shopping center in reverse. In its simplest form, the shopping center links two "magnet" department stores with a covered or enclosed mall, along which smaller specialty shops draw from the pedestrian traffic between, say, Macy's and Sears. The reverse, disposal version of this most American of building types is a dropping center. At one end, bags of miscellaneous trash get dropped into a trench from which a growing mound of sanitary landfill is fed. At the other end, items of possible utility—chairs, damaged furniture, rusty bikes, television sets, are dropped off and often reclaimed by folks finding treasure from other's discards. In between these major draws are rows of specialty containers into which one drops cans, cardboard, white glass, green glass, brown glass, plastic, and bundled newspapers. The cycle of consumption/disposal is here completed with a certain frivolity compensating for the bother of having to separate and

6.7. Garbage Drawing #25. Artist Mike Kelly finds treasure in trash, isolating images of garbage from Sad Sack cartoons to create his own art. *By permission of the artist.*

deposit all this stuff. Kids and adults alike can be seen flinging bottles into their designated containers, savoring the socially sanctioned smash at the end of each trajectory.

Garbage, Solid Waste

As is often the case, the words we use express our communal attitude toward what we are naming. Garbage means, in addition to discarded animal and vegetable remains, "anything contemptibly worthless, inferior or vile." We shouldn't have to touch it (or smell it), we throw into a chute, or bag it and leave it by the curb to be picked up by "garbage men." Although in some societies many people live from sorting through this refuse, we mostly try not to think about it.

For over 10 years, the New York City Department of Sanitation has had Mierle Ukeles as its artist-in-residence. Ms. Ukeles, a conceptual artist combining unusual personal sensitivity with a large measure of *chutzpah*, chose as her first "artwork" to personally shake hands with every single sanitation worker. As she traveled around New York to shake, un-gloved, the hands of over 7000 men, she sparked a kind of catharsis among them. Some cried, others told of being refused requests for water by residents put off by their smell, most were visibly moved.

Ukeles' next work consisted of encasing a solid waste collection vehicle (garbage truck) with mirrored panels, so that when people looked at it they saw their own reflection. Her crowning achievement in raising public awareness that we are, to some extent, what we throw away, was the recent *Garbage Out Front* exhibition at the Municipal Art Society's Urban Center. Containing educational exhibits on waste disposal, art from recycled materials, a cross-section through a landfill, and examples or architecture for waste disposal, the show attracted public officials, design professionals, sanitary engineers and interested citizens.

Calling this by-product of consumption "solid waste" transforms it into something approaching the variety and potential of the actual matter. "Leavings" might be an even better expression of its potential as a resource for recycling, mining materials, fuel, organic compost. There is an impressive amount of research, experimentation and commercial exploration around treating our leavings as a resource. From fueling the generation of electricity with old tires (the United States discards 250 million each year) to mining landfills for their valuable contents and fuel potential, we are finally confronting the problem and the opportunity. Architects can help.

6.8. Mierle Ukeles, artist-in-residence at the New York City Department of Sanitation, covered a collection truck with mirrors so that passersby could see their own reflection. *Photo: Courtesy of Ronald Feldman Fine Arts.*

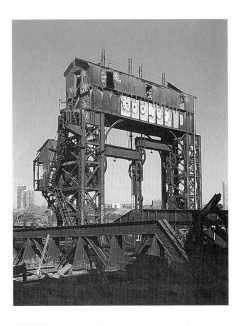

6.9. We casually discard structures of great beauty and significance. This former gateway to water-borne freight trains graces Manhattan's West side.

Civic Overseer

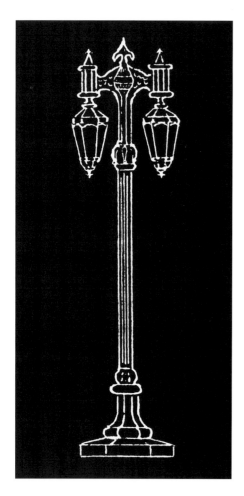

6.10. New York City Art Commission reviews all structures built on public land for appropriateness and visual quality. This design for a street lamp from their archive was approved in 1928.

New York City has had a unique institution overseeing the design of public architecture, public art, and almost anything else built on public land, since 1898, when the New York City Art Commission was formed. Possibly the oldest design review board in this country, it has held design in the public realm to a high standard for most of its tenure. The Commission has an advisory role to the Mayor (its offices are in the attic of City Hall, around the dome) and is usually comprised of an artist, an architect, a landscape architect, a layperson in the arts, and representatives of the Mayor, the Brooklyn Museum and the Metropolitan Museum of Art.

Every design for a work of art, public landscape or public architecture is first presented, in the preliminary design phase, to a design committee which engages the designer in a fairly rigorous dialogue about appropriateness, design intent, formal solutions, the materials and colors proposed. Preliminary designs are often revised, and sometimes rejected, based on this presentation. When the design is felt to be acceptable, it is presented to the full Commission for its vote. An accepted design receives a preliminary approval at this time, with one additional presentation required for final approval before construction.

The Art Commission has had a major impact in raising the level of public construction by its power of disapproving designs and by the constructive influence its hearings have had on the City agencies responsible for constructing public works—schools, fire and police stations, water works, prisons, sewage plants, parks and playgrounds. In an annual awards ceremony, it recognizes the best designs submitted in the past year. Certificates are given to the City agencies sponsoring the premiated projects as well as the designers, with the result that the construction agencies now compete for these awards, and encourage the architects they retain to produce winning designs, thereby raising the level of design for all public projects.

The author's participation in the design of the marine transfer stations and sludge dewatering facilities described in this section resulted from the requirement to obtain Art Commisssion approval. In both construction programs, the Art Commission suggested to the engineering firms responsible for the projects that an architect be added to the team to integrate these large structures into their neighborhoods and to give them an appropriately civic architectural character. Collaborating with four of the largest engineering firms in the region, the author had the privilege and pleasure of working on the kind of vast infrastructure projects which are seldom part of an architect's practice.

6.11. Sludge Dewatering Facility, 26th Ward, New York City (with Stone & Webster/Hazen & Sawyer, Engineers). *Photo © Roy Wright.*

6.12. Seal of the City of New York, New York City Art Commission Archive.

6.13. Sludge Storage Facility, Wards Island, New York City (with Stone & Webster/Hazen & Sawyer, Engineers). *Photo © Roy Wright.*

The plastic bag of New York garbage left by the curb (what is left after recycling cans, bottles, plastic, newspapers, batteries, etc.), has just been thrown under the metal mandible of the sanitation collection truck by one of the 7000 hands shaken by Ms. Ukeles (see p. 133). As soon as about two tons of similar bags are squeezed in, the truck heads toward one of the marine transfer stations (MTS) along the city's shoreline. After a long wait in a line of similar vehicles the truck drives up a ramp to the upper level of the MTS, backs up to a gap in the floor, and disgorges its load into an open barge waiting below. The filled barges, formerly dumped in the Atlantic, are currently towed by tugs to a vast sanitary landfill, growing in alternate layers of refuse and earth along Arthur Kill in Staten Island. When this man-made mountain reaches its final height in about 10 years, it will be the highest point in the city, and will require that some other way be in place for absorbing the 13,000 tons of trash which accumulate daily.

6.14. Marine Transfer Station, West 59th St. Refuse is "tipped" into barges, covered with a plastic mesh, and towed to the Fresh Kills Landfill on Staten Island where it accumulates at the rate of 13,000 tons per day (with Greeley & Hansen, Engineers).

6.15. Marine Transfer Station, W. 59th St. Tugboats nudge barges into their berth under the shed seen in the distance. The covered bridge at the right brings sanitation vehicles to the upper-level tipping floor.

6.16. Marine Transfer Station, W. 59th St. The main facade/entrance gate replicates the original nineteenth-century sanitation pier formerly occupying this site.

6.17. Marine Transfer Station, W. 59th St. The long elevation recalls the covered bridges of New England.

6.18. Marine Transfer Station, Greenpoint. A simple, "generic" design now utilized in a number of similar facilities (with EBASCO, Engineers).

6.20. Marine Transfer Station, West 59th St. Neon light sculpture by artist Steven Antonakos outlines these two sheds at dusk. On the building's north face, occasional windows glow with orange backlighting.

6.19. Marine Transfer Station, West 59th St. The visual language of industrial, waterfront sheds utilized in this Hudson River facility has its precedent in the ship piers formerly lining the entire shoreline of Manhattan (with Greeley & Hansen, Engineers).

6.21. Marine Transfer Station, West 135th St. Alternating bands of metal and translucent panels organize the building's facades (with Greeley & Hansen, Engineers).

6.22. Sludge Dewatering Facility, Tallman Island, Queens. Sewage sludge is reduced to its essence here and sent to storage and eventual composting (with Stone & Webster/Hazen & Sawyer, Engineers).

Human Waste

The great literature about the human condition, from Shakespeare to Freud, Norman O. Brown and Ernest Becker, has recognized the basic duality of man as a heroic being aspiring to divinity, yet simultaneously a creature with a mouth and an anus, having to daily eat, drink and eliminate to live. The contrast has long been a source of shame, amusement, irony and wonder to theologians, philosophers, psychologists and the rest of us. Human waste is, simply, another by-product of our existence on earth. In the words of a popular bumper-sticker, "shit happens."

The technology for disposing of human waste was understood at least as far back as the Minoan civilization on Crete. There are underground clay pipes for sanitary drainage in the Palace of Knossos, circa 1600 B.C., and both Chinese and Indian farmers recycle human waste (night soil) as fertilizer. Despite this, the world's populations have been surprisingly slow in treating and finding uses for human waste. Even in New York City, raw sewage from much of Manhattan flowed, untreated, into the Hudson River until 1987, when the North River Pollution Treatment Facility was built. (See Chapter 2, Riverbank State Park Case Study.)

Sludge Happens

Sewage treatment is the process of turning raw sewage into two end-products: a relatively clean liquid effluent which can be returned to the ground, a river or the ocean, and the semi-solid residue of the treatment process known as sludge. In its most prevalent form, the process entails collecting the product of countless drains; removing insoluble matter (sand, stones, tires, etc.); letting suspended solids settle to the bottom of, or float to the top of, tanks where oxygen-breathing (aerobic) bacteria feast on them; letting solids thicken in heated tanks where other bacteria (anaerobic) are at work in the dark; chlorinating and returning the treated liquid to a nearby waterway or underground water table; collecting the remaining sludge, and then . . .

Until 1988, when the U.S. Congress banned the ocean dumping of sludge, the sludge from New York City's sewage plants was pumped into large sludge barges, taken some 100 miles to a point in the Atlantic Ocean known as the New York Bight, and, together with New York's solid waste, dumped in. It was hoped that the depth of the ocean at this point, and its distance from land, would result in sufficient protection from contamination while nature did its work of recycling and purifying the dumped material. This long-standing practice was finally prohibited when studies of the ocean bottom indicated that the sludge resisted absorption, and garbage began to wash up on beaches along the Long Island and New Jersey coasts. Something different clearly had to be done about sludge. The projects which follow represent an interim stage in dealing with it.

Sludge Dewatering Facilities

New York City had previously dumped daily into the ocean enough sludge to cover a football field to a depth of over ten feet. Turning this volume of liquid waste into a material which could be handled and disposed of on land ultimately involved the construction of sludge dewatering facilities at eight of the City's 14 water pollution control plants. Built at a cost of $545 million in only 42 months, these structures were dewatering all the sludge by June of 1992.

The joint venture of Stone & Webster and Hazen & Sawyer, with Richard Dattner Architect PC as design architect, was asked by the NYC Department of Environmental Protection to design efficient, long-lasting structures utilizing the best currently available technology at existing sewage treatment plants in all five boroughs. NYCDEP mandated that the architectural treatment and landscaping of these large structures be as important as the process and engineering requirements. The new facilities were to be respectful of their neighborhood context and the special architectural character of each sewage treatment facility, many of which were important examples of WPA public architecture.

The process these buildings house is complex because of its scale and the nature of the material to be processed, but is conceptually as simple as a salad spinner. Sludge is piped to these buildings and is spun dry in high-volume centrifuges which remove most of the liquid component, cycle it back through the sewage treatment, and leave a moist, cake-like material called sludge cake. Belt conveyors carry the sludge cake to storage hoppers holding about one day's product located over truck bays from where the product is taken away. The design of the equipment, piping, ventilation, electric power, and supporting structure was the responsibility of the joint venture engineers. The architect's task was to design appropriate, attractive containers for this vast machinery which would minimize their visual impact and enhance their neighborhoods.

6.23. Sludge Dewatering Facility at 26th Ward, Brooklyn (right) feeds "sludge cake" to the storage facility in the foreground (with Stone & Webster/Hazen & Sawyer Engineers). *Photo © Roy Wright.*

6.24. Sludge Dewatering Facility, Wards Island, Manhattan. Odor control hoppers are visible through the window wall (with Stone & Webster/Hazen & Sawyer, Engineers).

Modular Design, A Kit-Of-Parts

The design of a number of similar facilities, within strict time limits and public spending constraints, suggested a strategy of modular, system design. As in the author's designs for New York City's prototypical intermediate schools (see Chapter 3, *Public Schools*), a "kit-of-parts" design approach emerged, with an important difference. Where the prototype intermediate schools utilize *modular buildings*—classroom wings, and a central administrative and shared activity core, the sludge treatment facilities are composed of *modular components*.

The "kit-of-parts" for these buildings consists of exterior construction elements rather than buildings, allowing for greater flexibility of interior layout to accommodate sludge processing systems of varying sizes. Exterior elements which can be combined in different ways allow for varied architectural designs to harmonize with surrounding neighborhoods and to respect the architecture of the existing treatment facilities. At the same time, the consistent design vocabulary created by these modular components visually unifies the disparate facilities and helps the public to recognize their existence, as well as understand their function and importance.

A Design Vocabulary

As five words can be combined to create dozens of intelligent sentences, five design elements are sufficient for a design vocabulary of surprising variety. Each component has a rationale for comprising part of the "architectural sentence" represented by each of the eight sludge dewatering facilities:

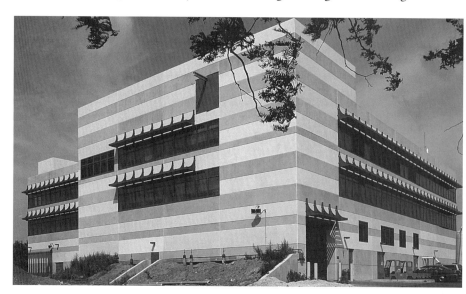

6.25. Sludge Dewatering Facility, Oakwood Beach, Staten Island. The inner workings of this vital facility are revealed to educate (and relieve the fears of) the public (with Stone & Webster/Hazen & Sawyer, Engineers).

6.26. Sludge Facilities, "Kit-of Parts."

6.26a. Precast Concrete Panels: most appropriate as the primary cladding material because of their strength and longevity without required maintenance. Wall panels are fabricated in several colors, with varied dimensions and scoring patterns. Wall surfaces are striated (parallel stripes, or striae), have a checkerboard pattern, or are framed in contrasting colors. Building panels are flat and rectilinear while curved panels enclose storage tanks and form a transition between ground and walls.

6.26b. Aluminum Cornice/Sun-shade Units: these components accomplish a variety of tasks and add three-dimensional interest to the facade. By adding visual richness, transparency and color to the palette of available materials, they help to visually integrate the new buildings to their older, more traditional adjacent buildings. Used over windows, they provide shade and add depth. In a reversed configuration, they create a cornice-like, traditional "top" for the elevations and cast shadows which enliven the facade. Their lightness both relieves and emphasizes the massiveness of the concrete structures.

6.26c. Modular Window Walls: this curtain-wall system of clear glazing provides natural light to areas of the building where people work or take breaks. Bands of windows emphasize the horizontality of the facilities, while large, multi-story window walls are used to modulate the large facades and express the tall interior spaces housing vertical tanks. The transparent walls allow the inner workings to be visible, helping to educate the public.

6.26d. Pyramid Skylights: at the point where stacks exit the building, these glazed pyramids allow sunlight into the facility, to benefit plant workers and to make the machinery more visible through the window walls. The stacks are part of the odor control system, and are frankly expressed as part of the industrial process.

6.26e. Earth Berms and Landscaping: a natural way to visually anchor each building to the site, and to bury part of the building to minimize its apparent scale. Landscaping with plants native to each site preserves and enhances its ecological balance. As these facilities are all located along natural waterways, and it has become New York City's policy to increase access to sewage plant sites for recreational use, this is an important design consideration.

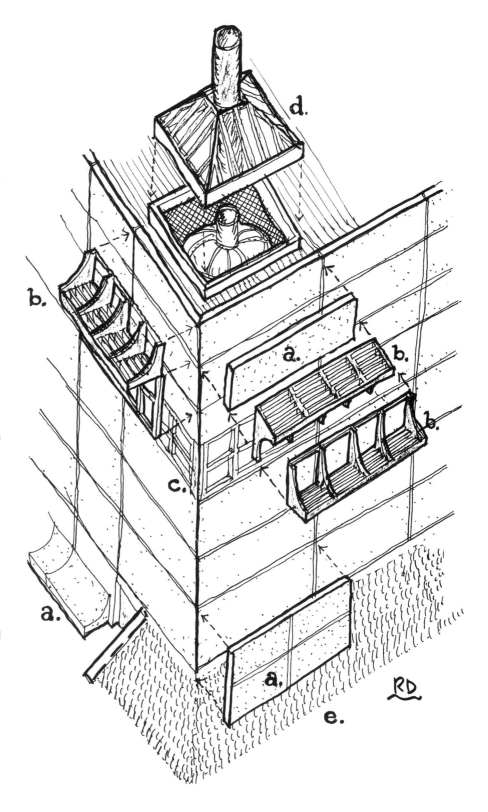

6.27. Map of New York City showing the location of the sludge treatment and storage facilities illustrated in this chapter.

6.28. Sludge Dewatering Facility, Oakwood Beach, Staten Island. Components from the "kit" were combined in different ways at each site to respond to each context (with Stone & Webster/Hazen & Sawyer).

6.29. Architect's sketch of the Oakwood
Beach facility. Seen from the nearby dunes, it
resembles a series of vast beach pavilions.

Sludge Dewatering Plants were built throughout the five boroughs at eight of the City's 14 sewage treatment plants. Three were built as prototypical "larger" plants, utilizing two rows of centrifuges. Five of the plants, containing a single row of centrifuges, are referred to as "smaller" facilities. At completion, they were supplemented by Sludge Storage Facilities to receive and hold the "sludge cake" product until the final composting step.

Oakwood Beach, Staten Island: The Gateway National Recreation Area—Miller Field and Great Kills Park—surrounds the Oakwood Beach Sewage Treatment Plant. The sludge facility is partly visible across an area of wetlands and sand dunes, and adjoins a community of former summer bungalows converted into year-round homes. Precast concrete panels, in alternating bands of off-white and warm gray, unify the four structures (two buildings, a circular tank, and a tower) into a slightly surrealist and oddly festive composition. Seen from the distant seashore they resemble over-scaled beach cabanas lost among the dunes.

6.30. Horizontal bands of alternating dark and light concrete panels unify this composition of building, tower and storage tank while reducing its apparent scale from the nearby community.

6.31. Wards Island Sludge Treatment Facility, Manhattan. Window wall enlivens the long north facade, reveals the facility's inner workings, and here reflects the Little Hell Gate Bridge beyond (with Stone & Webster/Hazen & Sawyer, Engineers).

Wards Island, Manhattan: This sewage plant was built under the WPA, with a formal, axial plan along which are sited monumental, somewhat classical buildings designed with a base, middle, and top. The sludge dewatering plant follows this formal precedent with a monumental, symmetrical main facade. The frame of darker concrete panels, multi-story window, and crowning cornice reinforce the importance of this primary facade visible from the Triborough Bridge. As in the great Victorian train sheds (and New York's tragically demolished Penn Station), a more modern, utilitarian mass is built behind this primary elevation. This long, lower section of the facility is characterized by a vast window wall revealing the odor control towers and stacks within the building. The Wards Island facility became the prototype for the two other "larger" facilities built at 26th Ward, Brooklyn and Hunts Point in the Bronx.

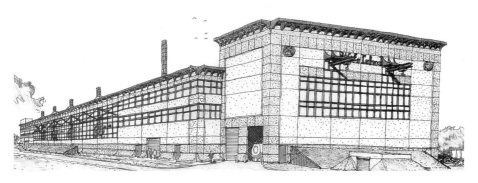

6.32. Architect's sketch showing landscaped berm anchoring building to the ground and reducing its apparent height.

6.34. Sludge Storage Facility, Wards Island, Manhattan. Storage facility (left) receives the product of the dewatering plant seen in distance (with Stone & Webster/Hazen & Sawyer, Engineers). *Photo © Roy Wright.*

6.33. Symmetrical front facade crowned by an aluminum cornice refers to the classical buildings of the adjoining WPA sewage treatment plant. Changing shadows cast by cornices animate the large concrete panel facades.

6.35. Sludge Dewatering Facility, 26th Ward, Brooklyn. Large expanses of window walls demystify the interior workings and help humanize this large structure (with Stone & Webster/Hazen & Sawyer, Engineers). *Photo © Roy Wright.*

6.36. An heroic architectural expression was considered appropriate for a huge civic facility serving millions.

6.37. Architect's sketch was closely realized except for two projecting derricks eliminated from the final design.

26th Ward, Brooklyn: Perhaps the most difficult of these buildings to integrate, this "larger" prototype adjoins the densely populated residential neighborhood housed in the large Starrett City apartment complex along the Belt Parkway. Several design strategies mitigate the apparent scale of this building: horizontal bands of contrasting concrete panels and bands of window walls with sun-shades enliven the facades; landscaped earth berms add natural color and texture while reducing the visual height of the structure; large expanses of multi-story window walls make the elevation facing the community more transparent and reveal the building's function. A decorative fence from the former facility is extended to visually integrate new and existing construction as well as screening portions of the site.

6.38. Contrasting horizontal bands and earth berms anchor the building and reduce its visual scale in deference to the nearby Starrett City residential community.

6.39. Sludge Dewatering Facility, Tallman Island, Queens. Overlooking the Throgs Neck Bridge, the building is seen here reflected in a sea of sewage settling tanks (with Stone & Webster/Hazen & Sawyer, Engineers).

Tallman Island, Queens: This site is at the shore of the East River just before it passes under the Bronx-Whitestone and Throgs Neck Bridges into Long Island Sound. Its limited site, between existing settling tanks and the bulkhead line, mandated plan modifications from the prototypical "smaller" design. The flatter, south elevation has a three-story window wall revealing the process equipment and allowing views through the narrow portion of the building. The north wall steps outward to take advantage of the wider part of the site, creating a more three-dimensional massing, unified by horizontal bands of dark gray concrete panels. The stepping also adds visual interest to the elevation seen from the two nearby bridges.

6.40. Architect's sketch: The stepping of the building mass necessary to fit the building to the difficult site helped break up the large volume and add visual interest.

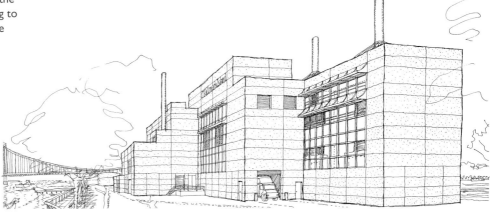

6.41. Seen from the East River, the stepped building closely follows the shoreline.

6.42. At the building's narrow end, large window walls allow views through the structure.

6.43. Sludge Treatment Facility, Bowery Bay, Queens. Typical of the smaller prototype facilities, it was designed to complement the adjoining WPA sewage treatment plant (with Stone & Webster/Hazen & Sawyer, Engineers).

Bowery Bay, Queens: This version of the "smaller" prototype is located on the Bowery Bay inlet of the East River, near La Guardia Airport. The existing sewage treatment plant is one of the WPA era, notable for a series of bas-relief friezes extolling manual labor, which often characterized the public architecture of that time. These sculptures were preserved, and the new facility pays homage to them by repeating a decorative band at a similar height around its base. If money had been available, a contemporary artist's version of this decorative treatment would have been a welcome addition, although most of the working figures would now have to be shown sitting at computer terminals rather than wielding shovels and wrenches. To add interest to the views from the adjoining residential community, two levels of sun-shade "eyebrows" modulate the facades, adding color and changing shadows.

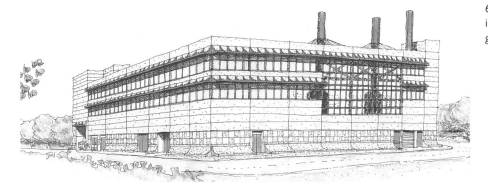

6.44. Architect's sketch. Like the building itself, these drawings were assembled from a graphic "kit-of-parts."

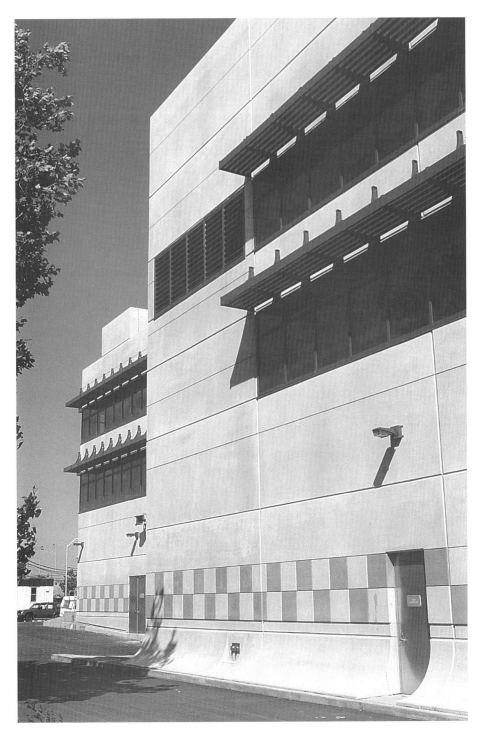

6.46. Aluminum sun-shade "eyebrows" minimize heat gain and cast changing shadows on the concrete facades. In reversed position (see the Wards Island Sludge Facility) these units become a decorative cornice.

6.45. The checkered pattern at the building's base echoes a band of heroic bas-reliefs extolling manual labor located at the base of the existing buildings.

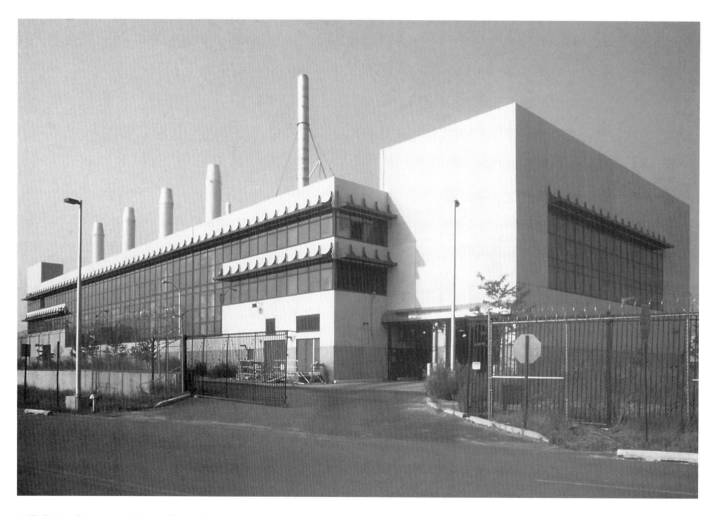

6.47. Sludge Dewatering Facility, Hunts Point, Bronx. This building, usually seen from a great distance, is the simplest variation of the larger prototype (with Stone & Webster/Hazen & Sawyer, Engineers). *Photo © Roy Wright.*

Hunts Point, Bronx: The third "larger" prototype is built along the East River shoreline of the Bronx. Its location away from residential communities, and the fact that it is visible primarily from a distance, suggested a simplified version of the Wards Island facility, without a cornice or other traditional features. Landscaped earth berms anchor this facility to its waterfront site, as the NYC Department of Environmental Protection has wisely required that native plantings be introduced at all these facilities to meet both esthetic and ecological needs.

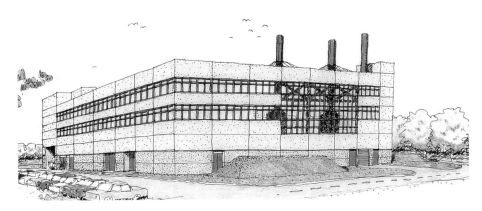

6.48. Architect's sketch of Jamaica Bay, simplest of the smaller prototypes.

Jamaica Bay, Queens: The first of the "smaller" designs, it became the prototype for the other four similar facilities. A location at the fringes of JFK Airport, among fuel tanks and utility buildings and away from any residential or sensitive natural site, eliminated the need for cornices, bands of color, or other special treatment. The limited site also allowed no space for berms or other landscaping. For that reason, this building became the simplest, "generic" version of the eight sludge dewatering facilities.

6.49. Sludge Dewatering Facility, Jamaica Bay, Queens. This building blends into a context of industrial buildings and fuel tanks bordering JFK Airport (with Stone & Webster/Hazen & Sawyer, Engineers). Cornice/sun-shades were eliminated from the "kit" for this building. *Photo © Roy Wright.*

Public Works Portfolio

New York State Thruway Rest Stop, Sloatsburg, NY: *Beyer Blinder Belle/Paul Gaiser Architects*. Rustic, picturesque architecture based on local mountain "camps" was used for the design of 16 sites operated by Marriott along this 550-mile toll road. Quarried stone, natural woods, simple plans and heroically scaled elements also recall railroad stations and the WPA lodges in our national parks.

6.50. While great variety is introduced in the 16 locations, a recognizable architectural language clearly communicates that this is a place of rest, food, and fun. *Photo © Patricia Layman Bazelon.*

6.51. A grand, vaulted ceiling restores some of the romantic and heroic imagery which formerly surrounded travel, and is now so seldom found. *Photo © Patricia Layman Bazelon.*

Ventilation Building, Charlestown, Massachusetts: *CBT/Childs Bertman Tseckares Inc*. A dignified structure balancing functional requirements for ventilation and emergency egress with the necessity of respecting the historic buildings of the Charlestown neighborhood. An example of civic responsibility for a community.

6.52. Red brick, buff trim, copper details and shapes recalling nearby chimneys integrate this large structure successfully into an urban context. *Photo © Peter Vanderwarker.*

6.53. Some passersby might see in this facade a huge, friendly face looking in astonishment at the amount of traffic constantly passing before it. *Photo © Peter Vanderwarker.*

Public Works Portfolio

JFK/UMASS MBTA Station, Boston, Massachusetts: *CBT/Childs Bertman Tseckares Inc.* An intermodal facility, connecting rail transit and buses under a highway interchange, is realized in a direct architecture appropriate to its civic function.

6.54. The curtain wall sun screen has some of the streamlined esthetic of the commuter trains passing below it. *Photo © Nick Wheeler.*

6.55. Station interiors are inviting and reduced to design essentials. Nothing confuses the directness of the circulation or station function. *Photo © Nick Wheeler.*

Public Utilities

7

Invisible Mending (Civil Fabric)

Think of a city as an oriental carpet of incredible richness. (A "gorgeous mosaic" evokes comparable variety, but implies countless individual tiles and misses the interrelatedness of the urban enterprise.) There is a warp of strong, underlying threads supporting the structure above, a weft of crossing threads creating a two-dimensional matrix, vertical loops and tufts providing color, texture, and depth—the third dimension. Flying above this city reveals some of its pattern, but misses the underground web of conduits, sewers, subways. There are additional, invisible webs of association, memory, personal connection. We normally walk or drive along the surface of this tapestry, more aware of the tufts, loops and spaces between than of the underlying matrix.

Now think of the architect as a weaver, mending a tear in the fabric or weaving a new section where a bare spot shows. If more architects would imagine themselves as weaving a section of a valuable heirloom, we might avoid the works of self-indulgence, banality and inappropriateness which mar so many communities. Buildings of banality would be avoided by the need to continue the richness and variety of the surrounding pattern. Respecting the surrounding weave would preclude inappropriate scale. Self-indulgence would be tempered by an understanding of the complexity, value and history of the tapestry.

Endlessly mending the same pattern is not the goal—that would be a prescription for stasis and a kind of death (see Ada Louise Huxtable's recent writing on Colonial Williamsburg). The carpet has to be continuously re-woven, renewed as it grows, wears out, and changes to meet new needs. In this imaginary place where architects are weavers, knowledgeable carpet lovers would select some to mend the tears and others to add to the pattern, so that weavers of talent would occasionally combine existing strands with a few new threads into an original pattern of beauty—a flower growing in a field.

7   Public Utilities

Sherman Creek State Park
Generating Civil Recreation

As we change from an industrial to a post-industrial society, we abandon structures of surpassing scale, intricacy and beauty such as blast furnaces, gas and water works, and generating stations. Representing the collective effort of thousands of individuals, these immense constructions have a nobility and visual power matched by few contemporary public buildings. Bereft of their intended function, they embody a poignancy commensurate with their former heroic quality. (The German photographers Bernd and Hilla Becher have, since 1957, superbly documented this vanishing landscape of blast furnaces, water towers, gas tanks, mine heads, and grain elevators.)

Finding a public use for these retired workhorses is a strategy for their preservation finding increasing acceptance; Seattle's Gas Works Park is an early and notable example. The Sherman Creek Generating Station was built in 1908 to serve Upper Manhattan, and was closed in 1970 when air-quality standards made the coal-fired boilers obsolete. In 1973, the first New York State Park to be located in New York City, Roberto Clemente State Park, opened directly across the Harlem River from Sherman Creek, and the State proposed a second park at this site. An architectural feasibility study determined that the structure and spaces were suitable for conversion to a community recreation building, and detailed plans were prepared.

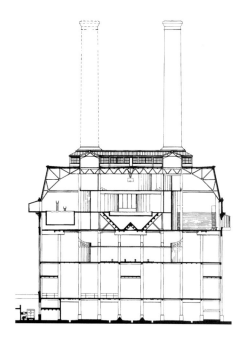

7.1. Sherman Creek State Park. Section: The unique cross-sections of coal-fired generating plants are suitable for present-day recreation. Original coal bunkers here support an indoor swimming pool.

7.2. Sherman Creek Generating Plant was closed in 1970 after rising air quality requirements rendered its coal-fired boilers obsolete.

7.3. Architect's sketch shows many existing features of the generating plant exploited for civic recreation along the Harlem River.

7.4. Over 100 feet high, the vast, skylit turbine room is one of the most spectacular interior spaces in New York. The light sconces along the wall are eight feet high.

7.5. Turbine room as park entrance gallery: a glass-roofed atrium entered by two wide ramps and new glass-enclosed elevators serving upper recreation levels.

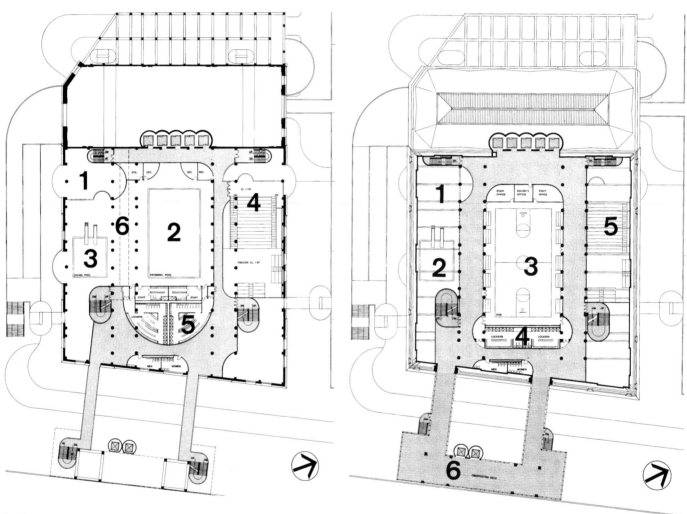

7.6. Swimming Level +116 Plan:
Key
1. greenhouse
2. swimming pool
3. diving pool
4. upper theater
5. lockers
6. observation corridor

7.7. Gymnasium/Observation Level +139 Plan:
Key
1. upper level of greenhouse
2. upper level of diving pool
3. gymnasium
4. lockers
5. upper level of theater
6. observation platform

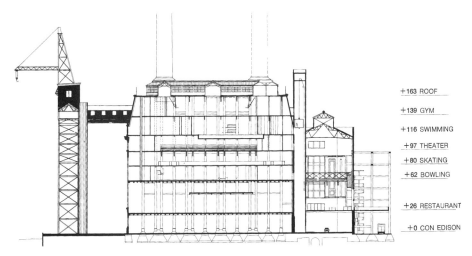

+163 ROOF

+139 GYM

+116 SWIMMING

+97 THEATER
+80 SKATING
+62 BOWLING

+26 RESTAURANT

+0 CON EDISON

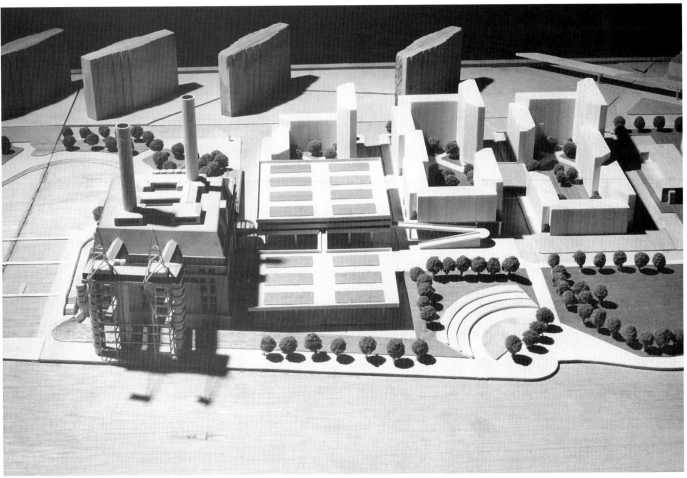

The 40-acre park site was to include a marina for 100 boats, a continuous waterfront promenade, and the restoration of several historic boat houses. The centerpiece would be the generating plant, rebuilt to house a wide spectrum of cultural and recreational functions. An indoor swimming pool would be fitted into the former coal hoppers, a skating rink and bowling alleys would occupy low-ceilinged spaces, and an experimental theater and a greenhouse would exploit the highest indoor spaces.

A political reversal, the growing awareness of the hazards of asbestos, and the recession of 1975 caused the abandonment of this project. Three years later, the State decided to locate its new park in the Hudson River, on the roof of an even larger building, the North River Pollution Treatment Facility. (See Chapter 2, Riverbank State Park.)

7.9. Restored generating plant as the core of a rebuilt neighborhood. Marina (at left) and riverfront amphitheater (at right) are linked by a landscaped promenade.

Civil Taxpayer

7.10. View from West 149th Street shows contrasting brick bands reinforcing the visual presence of this modest building surrounded by higher neighbors. Stainless steel canopy with flagpoles marks the public entrance. *Photo © Norman McGrath.*

One-story commercial buildings in New York City are called "taxpayers" because they usually cover the real estate taxes until they are demolished, in better economic times, for a larger building. One block from the West 149th Street "Hub" forming the commercial center of the South Bronx, this new customer service center for Con Edison is an important and permanent neighborhood fixture, paying taxes, providing local employment, and collecting payments for gas and electricity from community residents.

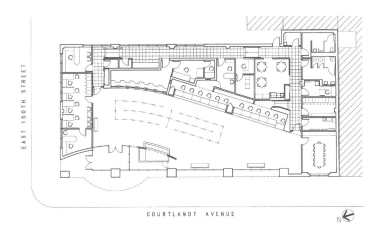

7.11. Plan: Simple rectangle has a curved public area carved out of it. Customer service representatives are stationed behind the continuous counter.

EAST 150TH STREET

COURTLANDT AVENUE

N

7.13. Entrance canopy is a visual beacon, marquee, and metal sculpture enlivening the masonry facade. *Photo © Norman McGrath.*

7.12. Interior is dignified and welcoming. The process of paying utility bills or reconciling accounts, seldom enjoyable, attempts to be pleasantly housed in a convenient location. *Photo © Norman McGrath.*

A low, modest structure, it nevertheless aims to express public accessibility, civic presence, and dignity with a palette of simple and inexpensive materials befitting a utility attempting to educate the public to conserve energy. A simple structural system of regular bays, large window areas, bands of contrasting bricks, and a stainless steel canopy utilize ordinary materials to create a sense of welcome and familiarity. The interior is organized to make the process of seeking assistance, or paying a bill, as effortless as possible.

Modest Civility

7.14. A humble material—concrete block—molded into a dignified structure on a modest budget. Each facade is treated differently to maximize energy conservation by this public utility. *Photo © Norman McGrath.*

Con Edison, a public utility serving the New York region, requested "a simple, functional design . . . avoiding any impression of wasteful expenditure of customers' money." (Not an inappropriate goal for most civic architecture in an age of diminishing resources—dignity on a budget!)

Located on Westchester Square, a busy urban node and commercial center in the Bronx, the building's two-story corner entrance matches the surrounding scale and is both highly visible and inviting. The exterior material is polished concrete block scored into 8-inch squares and accented by two lines of glazed orange brick. Exterior columns, exposed beams and railings are painted to contrast with the concrete block. Large panels of glass block enclose the two-story lobby.

Consistent with Con Ed's message of energy conservation, south-facing upper-level windows are shielded from the summer sun by an aluminum sunscreen, while first-floor windows are set back under a protective overhang. South and west facades of the lobby space are similarly shielded by deep overhangs. Windows on the north wall are set flush with the wall surface.

7.15. First Floor Plan: Customer service representatives and cashiers serve the public on this main level.

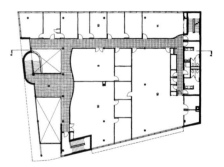

7.16. Second Floor Plan: Administrative functions and back office space occupy upper level.

7.17. Two-story entrance facing Westchester Square invites community residents to conveniently pay utility bills or seek other assistance. *Photo © Norman McGrath.*

7.18. South-facing Westchester Square elevation has projecting sun-screens to shield upper-level windows. Overhangs shield lower-level windows. *Photo © Norman McGrath.*

7.19. Two-story lobby makes the entire facility immediately legible to first-time visitors. *Photo © Norman McGrath.*

7.20. Customer service representatives behind an open, curving counter. Cash transactions are handled in a separate, protected area. *Photo © Norman McGrath.*

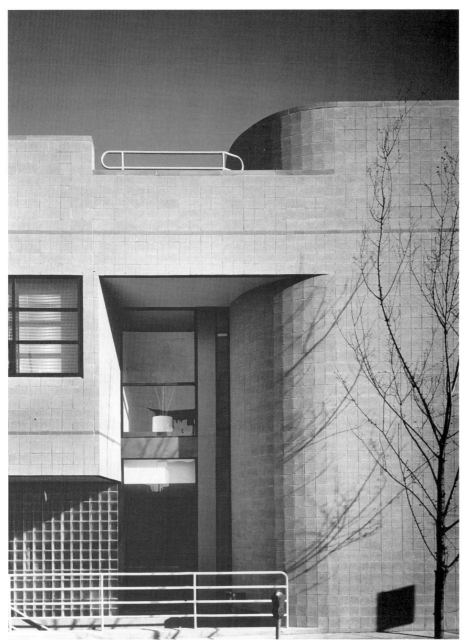

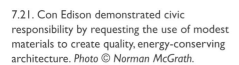

7.21. Con Edison demonstrated civic responsibility by requesting the use of modest materials to create quality, energy-conserving architecture. *Photo © Norman McGrath.*

7.22. Meter readers and investigators have a separate entrance to lower-level offices.

7.23. Riverfront promenade along the museum reveals an industrial landscape largely invisible to motorists hurtling along the overpass in the distance. *Photo © Strode Eckert.*

Oregon Museum of Science and Industry, Portland, Oregon: *Zimmer Gunsul Frasca Partnership Architects.* Grafting bold, new volumes to existing industrial structures along the Willamette River, this museum links the nineteenth century with the twenty-first. In many American cities, industrial waterfronts are a civic resource of incalculable value.

7.24. The museum is an assemblage of simple volumes at the water's edge, a lesson in solid geometry for kids and their parents. *Photo © Strode Eckert.*

7.25. Colonnaded central hall extends to form a monumental entrance portico. Rustication of split-face concrete block is a modern version of an ancient architectural treatment. *Photo © Paul Warchol.*

Water Resources Building, The Woodlands, Texas: *Taft Architects*. The first phase of a new civic center, this megaron-like building has a monumentality beyond its small scale. Simple materials and strong color establish a dignified palette for future development.

7.27. Public Board Room terminates the grand hall axis with an appropriately civic function. This building is a civilizing temple to small-town democracy. *Photo © Paul Warchol.*

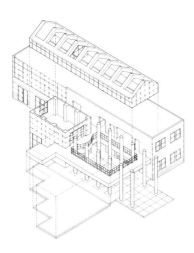

7.26. Water Resources Building. Axonometric: Echoes of ancient Greek temples lend a timeless presence to this civic center. Building is stepped along an adjoining river walk.

Temporary Air-Conditioning Plant, World Trade Center, NYC: *Davis Brody Associates Architects*. In the wake of the terrorist bombing, a temporary mechanical plant was put on-line in record time. The architect gave it a civic dignity commensurate with its essential function.

7.28. Industrial materials and exposed steel structure dignify this large urban artifact. Six months after its completion, this structure was disassembled. *Photo © Davis Brody Assoc.*

Public Utilities Portfolio

P. G. & E. Service Center, Geyserville, California: *Roland/Miller/Associates Architects.* The architect writes: "Gabled metal roofs, yellow and white paint, and clapboard siding . . . fit into the neighborhood, although it's obvious that something public is going on. . . . White pickets in the fence along the main street seemed appropriate; and all this was just fine with the locals who reviewed the design before we proceeded."

7.29. Customer service, operations office, work area and vehicular building are lined up "nose to tail" (in the designer's words) "along the highway." The simplicity and directness of these civic enclosures are more sophisticated than they initially appear. *Photo © Tom Rider.*

7.30. End elevation evokes the dignity and graphic clarity of a Grant Wood painting. *Photo © Tom Rider.*

Public Shelter

8

First, Do No Harm
(The Hippocratic Oath)

The architect has been compared to an orchestra conductor, a football quarterback, a master builder. Each simile aims to express the nature of the architect as leader of a team of specialists and coordinator of an undertaking of extreme complexity. There are even more compelling parallels between civic architects and general practitioners. Both deal with serious human issues of health and comfort involving complex systems of structure, circulation, environmental pressures. Both take responsibility for an entire organism (building) requiring the coordinated efforts of specialists and assistants within a setting of governmental regulations, codes, and stringent financial constraints.

This comparison is useful because it emphasizes the architect's responsibility to leave things better than they were found, to "first, do no harm." This is not as simple as it may sound. Imagine a recent public building you are familiar with—is it better than what it replaced, whether vacant lot or previous structure? Does it make your life easier, more pleasant, more full of delight? Is it healthy to work in or be near? Did it enhance its surroundings? Since it was built, do you feel better?

If the side effects of a prescribed treatment are worse than the problem, you stop the treatment and ask your doctor for another strategy of amelioration. Is it unreasonable to hold buildings, and architects, to a similar standard?

8   Public Shelter

Ridge Street Gardens, Manhattan, New York City
Civil Sanctuary

8.1. Ridge Street Gardens is a dignified addition to a run-down community undergoing gradual restoration.

One social consequence of our preoccupation with novelty is the neglect of the elderly among us. This category will eventually include most of us, and is therefore of more than academic concern. Relegating healthy older people to retirement communities or nursing homes impoverishes both the elderly and those they leave behind. One of the few Federal housing programs still active, albeit on a very small scale relative to the need, is the HUD 202 Program providing assisted housing for the elderly. Federal funds are made available to local, not-for-profit sponsors to develop, construct and operate modest residences for those not able to afford market level housing.

The New York Foundation for Senior Citizens is a leading 202 sponsor, having built several hundred apartments throughout the city. Its director, Linda Hoffman, with board member Zibby Tozer, exemplify administrators of unusual dedication who are willing to involve themselves in every aspect of planning, design, and construction along with the architect and builder. Ridge Street Gardens is an example of such a collaboration.

The seven-story building houses 100 apartments (75 one-bedroom, 24 studios, and one superintendent's unit) in a simple, linear structure dignified by a columned entrace canopy. The social center of the building—entrance lobby, lounge, dining room and kitchen—is clustered around the intersection of the entrance and the elevators, the busy focus of daily activity. An attendant at the lobby security desk monitors the entrance, assists residents, and is electronically linked to each apartment.

8.2. First Floor Plan: Social service functions are concentrated on this main level.
Key:
 1. vestibule
 2. lobby
 3. security desk
 4. lounge
 5. office
 6. dining room
 7. kitchen
 8. pantry
 9. efficiency apartment
10. one-bedroom apartment
11. superintendent's apartment
12. service lift
13. garden

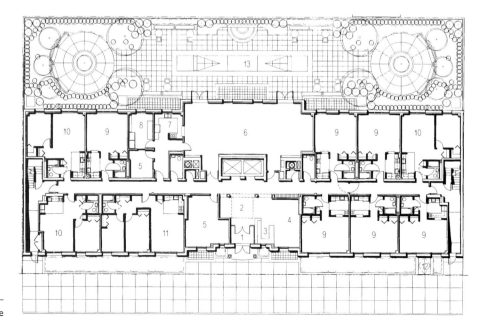

8.3. One-Bedroom Apartment: HUD regulations limit these units to 540 sq. ft.

8.4. Efficiency Apartment: These 415-sq.-ft. units comprise 25 percent of the apartments.

8.5. Resident lounge (above left). For residents with limited mobility, these sitting spaces on the entrance level provide opportunities for socializing. The control desk is a lively social center.

8.6. (above) The sponsor requested "Park Avenue interiors" within the modest budgets available to furnish these social spaces.

8.7. (left) Dining room houses social functions, resident meetings and an assisted dining program. In good weather, large doors open to adjoining garden.

Perhaps the most unique aspect of this residence is the care lavished on the interiors of these communal spaces. Within a tight budget (in the sponsor's words, "Park Avenue interiors, at Lower East Side prices"), Linda Hoffman and Zibby Tozer lovingly furnished these rooms as if they were their own apartments, providing the residents with a much-appreciated, home-like setting. The enclosed garden is designed with a comparable attention to detail, with game tables, seating, and a variety of trees and flowers cared for by the residents. A decorative fountain forms the centerpiece of this sunny, protected cloister.

8.8. Clinton Gardens. Architect's challenge is to create dignified, interesting design within extremely circumscribed requirements and limited budgets.

Built by the sponsor of Ridge Street Gardens, this apartment building for low-income elderly residents responds to a differing requirement for community context. A site smaller than that of Ridge Street, and special zoning preserving the character and scale of the Clinton neighborhood, mandated a ten-story building with a setback at the seventh floor to match the scale of West 54th Street.

The smaller building footprint limited ground floor space, requiring the dining room, kitchen, arts and crafts spaces, and laundry, to be located in the basement. By excavating the garden level one floor below grade, the basement became a second ground floor, thereby providing sunlight into the communal spaces and direct access from these spaces to the enclosed, south-facing garden.

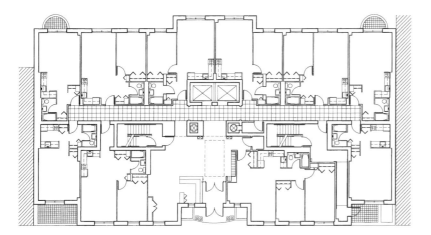

8.9. First Floor Plan: Site conditions mandated location of dining room, kitchen, and garden on the level below this entrance level.

8.11. Dignified entrance canopy identifies the residence, shelters the entrance, and enlivens the street.

8.10. These gardens are a vital extension of the social spaces within the building. Seating, game tables, shuffleboard, raised flower beds, and a fountain provide activity and visual delight.

Both Clinton and Ridge Street Gardens house extensive social service programs. Communal meals are served daily for those residents unable to prepare their own. Residents who are frail receive assistance with shopping, cooking and other household tasks. A small beauty parlor is a popular amenity, as are a variety of classes and social activities which help residents organize their days and remain active.

Civil Refuge

8.12. The Yonkers campus of Leake & Watts, designed by Frederick Law Olmsted, has served orphaned children since 1896.

Private charitable institutions have been providing public refuge for hundreds of years. As social needs grow beyond the means of private munificence (New York State's 1993 Department of Social Services budget is over $30 *billion!*), the boundaries between private philanthropy and public social welfare become increasingly permeable. As efficient and experienced providers of social services, private agencies are receiving increasing amounts of public funding.

Leake & Watts was established as an orphanage in 1831, as part of the Trinity Church Parish in a former time of immigration, disease, social dislocation, and urban poverty. Thousands of children have been raised to responsible adulthood at Leake & Watts; some former residents are now staff members. Current residents are orphans of a different sort. Primarily African-American teen-agers with living parents, they are often orphaned by crack-addicted mothers and jailed or otherwise absent fathers. Many are placed with relatives or in foster homes administered by Leake & Watts, while the most needy of refuge and socialization live and attend school on the historic Yonkers, New York campus.

Security and socialization are the major design determinants. A series of "worlds" of increasing socialization and responsibility is delineated within the nine new residential cottages, two rehabilitated cottages and new school. Residents are housed in single or double rooms; seven residents and staff make up a living unit occupying one wing of the upper floor of a cottage; two living units share a 14-resident cottage. Residents clean their rooms, prepare meals, and are responsible for other household tasks. Increasing responsibility earns residents increasing freedom and "points" which function as currency at the "B-Mod" store.

Three cottages comprise a village clustered around a shared village green. Front porch "stoops" form a transition between cottage and village. The three new villages and the two restored cottages house 154 residents on the Olmsted-designed grounds. Mature trees, stone walls, and other site features are carefully preserved. The orderly layout, serene landscape, and views of the Hudson River create a refuge from urban chaos for the average 18-month tenure of a resident.

8.13. Residential Cottage, Lower Level: Living and dining rooms, spare bedroom (for ADA compliance), kitchen, and laundry room are on this entrance level.

8.14. Residential Cottage, Upper Level: Each of two wings houses seven residents in single and double bedrooms. Resident staff at the central atrium monitor activity on both levels.

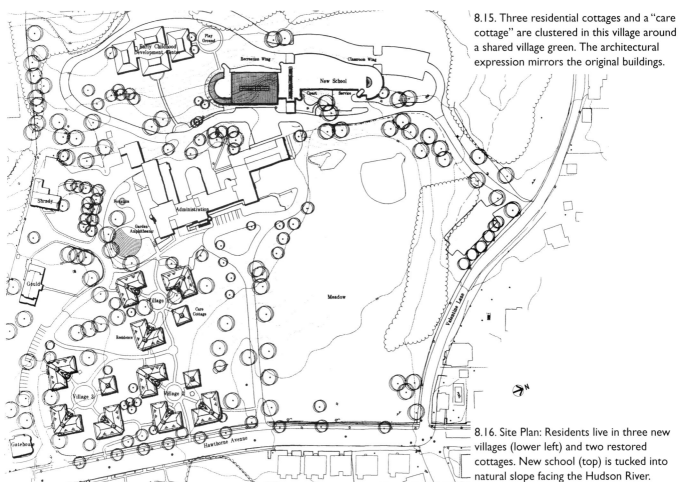

8.15. Three residential cottages and a "care cottage" are clustered in this village around a shared village green. The architectural expression mirrors the original buildings.

8.16. Site Plan: Residents live in three new villages (lower left) and two restored cottages. New school (top) is tucked into natural slope facing the Hudson River.

Schooling for Civility

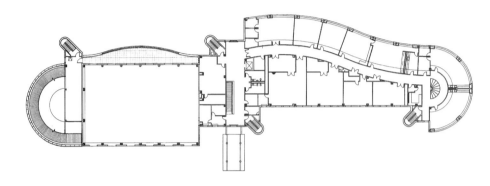

8.17. School, Upper Level: Science laboratories and shops occupy north wing (right); south wing houses upper levels of multi-purpose auditorium and gymnasium.

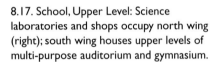

8.18. School, Middle Level: Classrooms and administrative offices occupy north wing; south wing (left) houses gymnasium and multi-purpose auditorium.

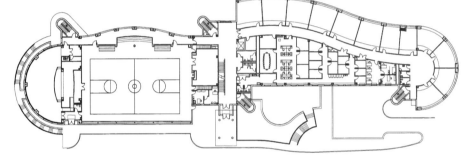

8.19. School, Lower Level: Classrooms, cafeteria (with outdoor terrace) and kitchen occupy north wing; swimming pool, lockers, and game room (with "B-Mod" store) in south wing.

The functional core of the Leake & Watts community is a new school tucked into a hillside behind the original orphanage which serves both the residents and additional pupils with special needs from the surrounding community. The curved facades of the school mimic natural site contours, soften the impact of the new building, and allow most classrooms to face the river. A central spine divides the school into a north wing containing classrooms, laboratories and shops, library, offices, and dining facility, and a south wing housing the gymnasium, swimming pool, lockers, student center and multi-purpose auditorium. The social and sports activity spaces function independently after school hours, and are available for community use.

8.20. Curved school walls follow natural contours of the site, minimizing site disruption and maximizing river views from classrooms.

8.21. New school (left) is below the existing administrative building (right) to preserve river views. Future bridge will link both facilities.

8.22. Architect's sketch showing new school linking existing administration building and early childhood center.

A City In A Building

8.23. Riverside Park Community. Maximizing efficient use of this site, the roof of I.S. 195 is the landscaped open space for the residential structure above. *Photo © Norman McGrath.*

In a time when even a small subsidized residence is difficult to develop, it might be helpful to consider a time when government-assisted housing was creating significant numbers of apartments each year, the final years of the Federal 236 Program. By the end of the 1960's, so many new schools and housing units were being planned that the New York City Educational Construction Fund (ECF) was created to acquire and develop sites for projects combining schools with either residential or commercial structures.

The largest single ECF building combined the 1200-unit Riverside Park Community, with Intermediate School I.S. 195 for 1800 students and a 350-car parking garage, quite literally a city in a building. (As timidity characterizes our present situation, a disregard for appropriate scale characterized that generation. Efforts to reduce the size of the project were rejected on the basis that housing was so desperately needed that any site available should be developed to its fullest potential. Somewhere between these extremes is an appropriate approach to resolving the housing needs of the poor.)

The major design challenge was breaking down the building into elements of human scale. The residential structure was divided into five individual towers organized along an octagonal, interior residential "street." These towers step in height from 11 to 33 floors, enclosing a south-facing courtyard and exploiting the magnificent Hudson River views to the south and west. One side of this "street" opens to the landscaped recreation plaza on the roof of the school below. Individual residential lobbies and communal spaces—library, meeting rooms, laundry rooms—populate this interior link and keep it safe.

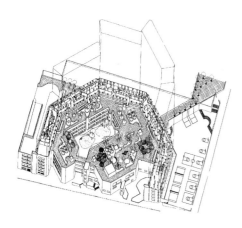

8.25. Axonometric of school roof and apartment lobby level. Internal "street" links five towers to two main building entrances.

8.24. Internal "street" overlooking landscaped courtyard links lobby entrances of the five residential towers. Service level below also opens to courtyard to enhance tenant security. *Photo © Norman McGrath.*

8.26. View of Riverside Park Community from the north. The octagonal form breaks up the large mass and maximizes river views for residents.

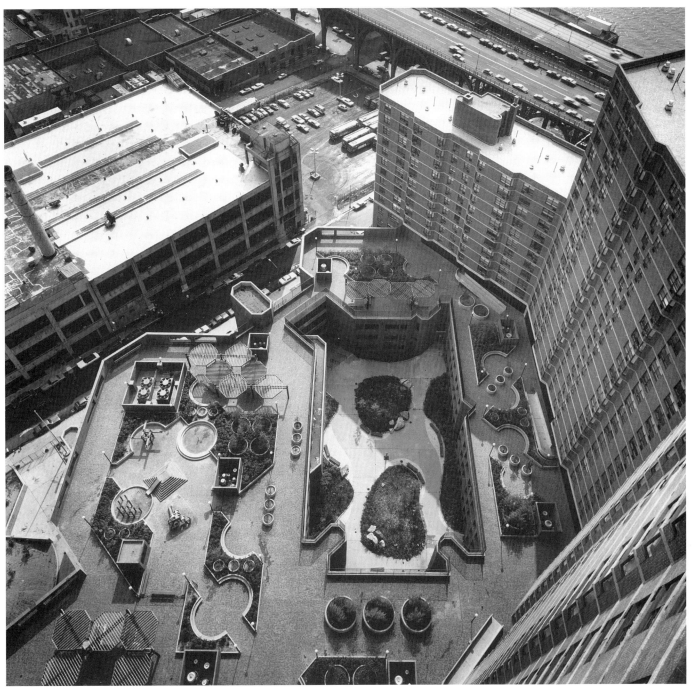

8.27. Apartments look out to the Hudson River over the residential courtyard on the school roof. Enclosed school courtyard (center) provides light and views for classrooms. *Photo © Norman McGrath.*

8.28. School courtyard is a protected cloister shutting out street traffic and noise. Most classrooms face this garden. Classes are held here in good weather.

The school is completely separate from the housing, organized with classrooms around an interior, landscaped courtyard protected from the surrounding industrial buildings and adjacent municipal bus garage. Ten student academies create smaller social units as the basis for the children's daily experience. Shared facilities—auditorium, library, gymnasium, cafeteria, etc.—are in a self-contained section available for after-school community use.

8.29. Auditorium is divisible by a motorized wall into a smaller auditorium and two lecture rooms. *Photo © Norman McGrath.*

8.30. Gymnasium is divisible by a motorized wall into boys' and girls' gyms. *Photo © Norman McGrath.*

Public Shelter Portfolio

CEPHAS Housing, Yonkers, New York: *Duo Dickinson Architect.* Fifteen units of permanent housing for the homeless are organized as vertical townhouses. Residential scale and materials help succesfully integrate assisted housing into a community.

8.31. Sloping site allows townhouses to be stacked without requiring an elevator. Although a six-story building on the downhill side, it retains the scale and visual texture of existing homes adjoining the site. *Photo © Mick Hales.*

8.32. A project in harmony with its community contrasts with a previous generation of public housing seen in the background. *Photo © Mick Hales.*

Singles Housing, Bronx, New York: *Skidmore Owings & Merrill Architects.* Transitional housing for three populations—the mentally ill, substance abusers and persons with AIDS—respects community scale as well as its own population. The sad irony here is that this transitional housing is in most cases superior to the permanent housing into which the residents are destined.

8.33. Corner rotunda is entrance and control point for residents. Two-story lounges expressed on the street facades add visual variety and modulate the scale of this civic shelter. *Photo © Whitney Cox.*

8.34. First Floor Plan: Prototype transitional residence is flexible enough to fit a variety of urban sites.

8.35. Two-story lounge and adjoining communal kitchen form the social center of an eight-unit cluster. Tall, operable windows make this a spacious-feeling, cheerful space. *Photo © Whitney Cox.*

Public Shelter Portfolio

Harbor Point, Boston, Massachusetts: *Goody, Clancy & Associates/Mintz Associates, Architects.* Boston's Columbia Point—one of the grimmest housing projects of its time—was radically renovated and supplemented with new townhouses and mid-rise apartments. The result is a superlative community of mixed income exploiting long-neglected harbor views. Harbor Point offers proof that design intelligence and political will can restore the most damaged setting. It is 95% rented, and is one of the lowest crime areas in the city.

8.36. Existing and new structures, high-rise and mid-rise, apartments and townhouses, are all mixed in this revitalized neighborhood. *Photo © Anton Grassl.*

8.37. Columbia Point at its low point. These large projects once represented a serious attempt to provide large numbers of housing units for the poor. Now that we have learned how to better design for this need, we require a housing program commensurate with the scale of the problem. *Photo © Goody, Clancy & Associates.*

Public Safety

9

Who Is Right? (The Rabbi Story)

The bewildering diversity of design approaches in a world with six billion inhabitants creates a need by architects to choose among competing dogmas which reduce that terrifying multiplicity to a simpler system, a "style" which can be named and understood by both practitioners and the public. Perhaps the question most asked of architects by non-professionals is: Who is right? Which is the correct philosophy of design? By way of response, one of the author's favorite stories is offered, transformed from the most commonly encountered version only by changing the profession of the disputing parties.

Two architects have deeply disagreed. One feels that all buildings should be white to best show the abstract beauty of their form, the other is convinced that buildings in different colors will more appropriately reflect the variety of uses and users. They decide to take their dispute to the most learned Rabbi in their community. The Rabbi agrees to hear their case and asks each, in turn, to present his arguments. The first architect, forcefully and with great logic and organization, presents the arguments for his position. After his presentation is complete the Rabbi, moved by brilliance of the argument, declares that the first architect is right.

The second architect is outraged, his position has not even been heard! The Rabbi relents and gives the second architect his full attention. The arguments for the alternative position pour forth, increasing in their eloquence as time wears on. At last, the second architect is done. The Rabbi, visibly moved by this presentation as well, declares that the second architect is right!

This declaration causes great confusion among the parties, not least with the Rabbi's wife, a woman equally wise and learned, who has been listening to the entire proceeding. She now leaps to challenge the Rabbi, exclaiming: "They can't both be right!" The Rabbi turns to his wife, his face full of the terrible burden of his calling, and says: "You too are right!"

9

Public Safety

New York City Police Academy, Bronx, New York City
Politia and *Polites*

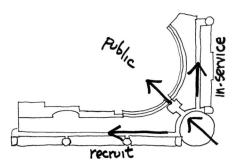

9.1. Police Academy is organized along three axes passing through a common entrance rotunda: public axis, recruit axis, in-service axis. Circulation for each user group is unambiguous and comprehensible.

When New York City sought a design for its new Police Academy, a major mandate was balancing the needs of both police (*politia*) and citizenry (*polites*). Both words are derived from the Greek *polis* (city), showing how closely the concepts of maintaining order and citizenship were linked in the Greek lexicon. The author's entry illustrated and the Ellerbe/Becket/Fieldman design were the two finalists, embodying contrasting views of appropriateness and civility which split the jury. In the words of the jury chairman, "The choice was: should the building fit in (the Dattner design) or stick out (the Ellerbe design)? We ultimately decided it should stick out." The Ellerbe submission was awarded first prize.

The Open Fortress
The author's design represented a conscious balance between police and community, respecting the low scale of the Grand Concourse neighborhood and providing community access to the playing field/parade ground, while providing a clear distinction between the building's functional sections. In character, the building is an open, permeable fortress, recalling familiar historic precedents such as armories, urban college campuses, and parade grounds. Expressive of its civic importance, it nonetheless "fit in" to an urban fabric which has long distinguished this part of the Bronx.

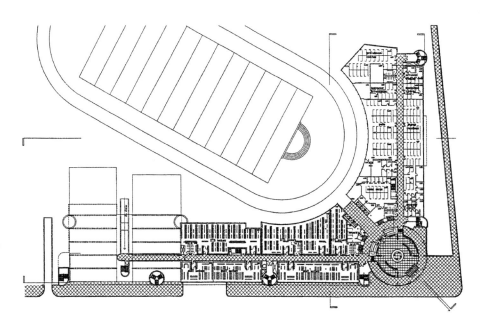

9.2. Entrance Level Plan: Police Academy both defines surrounding streets and encloses a parade ground and playing field available for community recreation. Recruits muster daily under the overhanging recruit wing.

9.3. Architect's sketch of the proposed Academy from the Grand Concourse, a neighborhood landmark in harmony with a historic neighborhood.

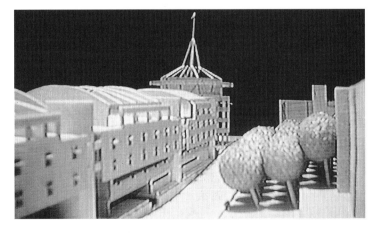

9.4. Corner rotunda defines the main entrance, serves three user axes, and anchors the facility to the street grid.

9.5. View of scale model along bordering street taken with miniature TV camera. New tools allow communities to accurately gauge visual impacts of proposed facilities.

The intersection of East 153rd Street and Concourse Village West is the closest point to the Grand Concourse. A round entrance tower at this corner clearly defines the primary entrance for public, recruits, in-service personnel and staff. Parking, storage, receiving and firing ranges are located on lower levels, raising the open field to the level of the surrounding streets.

Having entered through a common entrance lobby, the three major user groups each have a clearly defined direction. The recruits turn left into the longest, "straight and narrow" building wing exemplifying the greatest order and discipline. In-service personnel (police officers taking advanced courses) turn right into a more complex and varied wing. The public follows the central axis into the parade ground, or uses the other central, publicly accessible spaces in the round tower—auditorium, lecture room, and Police Museum. A roof-top observation platform topped by a communications mast, satellite dishes and microwave antennas provide a neighborhood landmark and scenic overlook open to the neighborhood.

9.6. Curved interior elevations surround the running track. Like New York's Finest, a protective, somewhat rigid exterior yields to a gentler, freer interior—a tough cop with a heart of gold.

9.7. View from the Concourse. Straight and narrow recruits' wing (left) and in-service wing (right) meet at the entrance rotunda. Communications masts and a public overlook make this a community landmark.

9.8. Entrance rotunda combines public plaza, control point, and exhibit space. Openness of this space stresses the Academy's links to the community.

Civil Progression

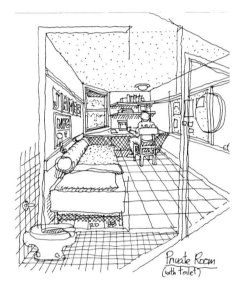

9.9. Private Room: The progression to increasing levels of socialization (and liberty) begins here. Respecting the resident's humanity might help that person learn to respect the humanity of others.

Perhaps the most terrible manifestation of our present social disorder is the violent crime being committed by children, often against other children. (I use "children" in the nominal sense, more accurate is the title of Alex Kotlowitz' book about life in the Henry Horner Housing Project in Chicago, *There Are No Children Here*.) Children arrested for serious crimes need an environment which is safe and coherent, strictly and fairly run, to nurture whatever spark of socialization and humanity has survived. (Those sociopaths with no such potential will have to be isolated for the safety of their more hopeful peers and the rest of us.)

In this proposal for the New York City Youth Center, increasing levels of self-control and responsibility earn residents access ("keys") to spaces of increasing socialization. Real keys are given to each resident for their own room to reinforce a sense of self. Responsible behavior can earn incremental access to: a House shared by 16 residents and staff; a Commons shared by three Houses; and the interior Main Street serving the entire facility. A Front Porch forms a transition between House and Commons, and a Neighborhood Porch links the Commons to the Main Street. These transitional spaces help define territory and provide additional levels of responsibility and freedom.

9.10. House: Shared by 16 residents and staff, this social group acts as family in the learning of appropriate behavior, which is rewarded by increasing levels of liberty.

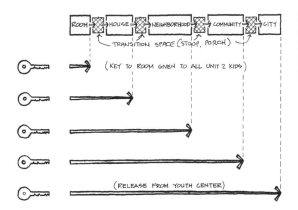

9.11. "Keys" to increasing choice and liberty are earned by learning socialized, responsible behavior. Transition spaces between each level define territory and provide additional levels of responsibility and freedom.

Commons - "Neighborhood"   RD '88

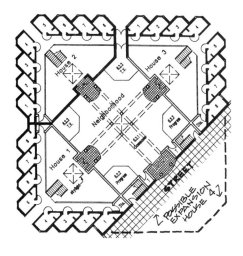

9.12. Commons: Corresponding to a neighborhood, this space is shared by three houses linked to the commons by transitional "front porch" spaces. Responsible residents practice interacting non-violently in larger groups with a greater range of freedom.

9.13. Basic planning unit of commons, three houses, and 42 rooms form residential clusters along a "main street" circulation spine.

9.14. Main Street: Linking residential clusters to processing areas, school, dining facility and gymnasium, this secure, lively, skylit mall provides a level of freedom approximating (for some residents, exceeding) that of the "real world" outside.

Orland Park Village Center, Orland Park, Illinois: *Perkins & Will.* These structures recall the clarity and monumental simplicity of early twentieth-century civic structures by Alvar Aalto and Eliel Saarinen. They express the function of government as important, welcoming and open to public view.

9.15. (left) "Scandinavian" architectural forms are surprisingly appropriate to the American heartland. *Photo © Nick Merrick/Hedrich Blessing.*

9.16. (right) Reflecting pool adds a calm dignity to a modern civic center. *Photo © Nick Merrick/Hedrich Blessing.*

9.17. Entrance pavilion links administration wing (at right) with police administration (at left). The council chamber, as the primary town meeting hall, occupies a place of honor between the two wings and rises above them. *Photo © Karl Backus.*

Bensalem Township Municipal Facilities, Bensalem Township, Pennsylvania: *Bohlin Cywinski Jackson Architects.* The simplest of design concepts here results in a most elegant public building. Two rectangular single-story wings—one for police, the other for town administration—are hinged at the higher volume of the ceremonial council chamber. A glass pavilion links the two blocks while offering views of the woodlands beyond.

9.18. Council chamber, entered from the entrance pavilion, is both inviting and monumental. A gently curved enclosure distinguishes this ceremonial space from the rectilinear administrative blocks. *Photo © Karl Backus.*

Public Safety Portfolio

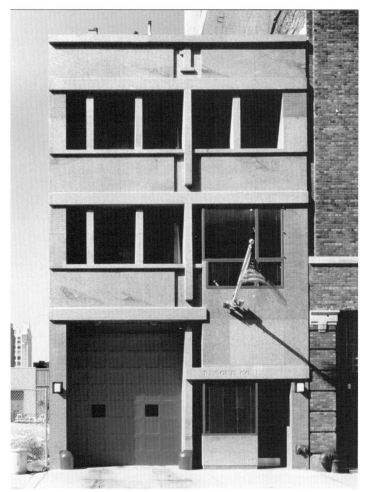

Rescue Company 1, New York City: *The Stein Partnership Architects.* This new facility for the oldest fire rescue company in the U.S. has the simplicity and directness of a piece of fire-fighting apparatus. A powerful civic presence for a building only 25 feet wide.

9.20. Stone work from the original facade is incorporated into the firefighters' dining room and social center on the first floor, a history lesson sadly not visible from the street. *Photo © Eduard Hueber.*

9.19. Street facade manages to be dignified, strong and whimsical at the same time. When the overhead door opens, the equipment inside fascinates passersby. Firefighters sleep on the upper levels. *Photo © Eduard Hueber.*

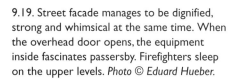

9.21. First Floor Plan:
Key:
1. house watch
2. apparatus room
3. decontamination area
4. coat room
5. dining/kitchen

10

What's New? (Civil Novelty)

That is the question at the center of our interest and concern. It is a ubiquitous greeting, song title, raison d'etre of magazines, television specials, books. Change is noticed, exciting, an antidote to the boredom of the everyday, the spice of life. A change of costume ("look") adds a new dimension to a human body essentially unchanged for millennia. The urge to transcend, or disguise, the physical limits of our being is as old as history. We dress up (or dress down) to look smarter (dumber), sexier (slouchier), fiercer, powerful, with-it. At night we take off our outer layer of protection, projection, signifier of status, and we go to bed.

Architects also concern themselves with the new, but the time frame is (or, at least, was until fairly recently) several orders of magnitude removed from that of costumes. In Roman times architectural features changed over centuries. Medieval cathedrals changed over the decades of their construction as master masons came, went or died, and others took their place, bringing ideas and techniques from other sites. The advent of the book brought the possibility of widely distributing illustrations of the latest design developments. Architectural magazines now provide high-quality color photographs of new projects within months of their completion, sometimes even before their completion. Our appetite for the new is fed by an ever-increasing number of images. Why are we still hungry? What is the problem?

The appetite for the new is insatiable: the new quickly becomes familiar; the familiar is no longer new; so what else is new? For reasons of survival, eyes and brains in living creatures evolved to instantly recognize motion, change, newness. The first priority is to be aware of some new situation in our environment that might threaten our survival. The problem is that the constantly changing new data "overwrites" other information equally or more important to modern urban life.

We are masters of the ephemeral, at the cost of a diminished ability to focus on events that unfold in the long term. In public architecture, where projects can take five to 15 years between concept and realization, and buildings can last for centuries, newness is in conflict with other design goals: integrity, respect for context, economy of means (conserving resources), civic continuity. Originality is a more appropriate category than newness. It suggests the most creative solution to a problem rather than the novelty of the merely new; it is a category with a longer shelf life.

Public Assembly

Democratic National Convention 1992, New York City
Civic Platform

10.1. Banner graphics transform the neighborhood around Madison Square Garden. (Convention graphics by Bill Anton and Gina Russell.) *Photo: DNCC.*

"And then, as good, better even, when the camera cuts to Macy's basement—to Macy's basement! and my my, and oh ah, the improbable, improvised venues of history!—where the Clintons kiss, hug and jig till it's time to . . . emerge into the Garden and the miraculous, swirling, focused shower of silver waiting for them. . . . It was wonderful and it was pure; a current event, however transitory, of the felt moment." (Stanley Elkin, *The New York Times*, July 19, 1992)

Elsewhere in this book are described public projects designed to serve their users for generations. Taking their cues from surrounding neighborhoods, serving as settings for learning, recreation, waste disposal, or sewage treatment, built of concrete, masonry or steel, these structures are tangible and reasonably permanent. In the late summer of 1991, along with several other New York architects, we were interviewed for a project which would be the antithesis of permanence and local contextuality, the Democratic National Convention to be held in Madison Square Garden for four days in July of 1992.

The architect selected would work with the Democratic National Convention Committee (DNCC), The City's Economic Development Corporation (EDC), and a cast of hundreds to create a setting for four days of business meetings, speeches, caucusing, voting, giving interviews, more speeches, electing a candidate, celebrating a ticket, and communicating to the tens of millions of television viewers a party platform and the persons embodying that platform.

A Design Collaboration

The firms interviewed jointly by DNCC and EDC had been selected for their record of successfully completing public projects of comparable complexity and time constraints. Although politics did not play a part in the selection (our team had Democrats and Republicans on it, and no one asked), we felt it important that our team reflect the cultural diversity which would be an important theme of the Convention.

The DNCC had already selected a producer (Gary Smith) to direct the performance aspects of the convention, assisted by a stage designer (Rene Lagler) who had designed the 1988 Convention in Atlanta. To secure the 1992 Convention and the economic benefits flowing from that event, New York City and the non-partisan NY92 Committee offered a package of construction, security arrangements, communications and amenities costing over $20 million. Part of that package, under the direction of EDC, was the design and construction of the podium, press stands, camera platforms and other temporary facilities which would transform the Garden into the center of the world's attention for four days.

10.2. Podium design had to balance visibility, access, security, lighting, and camera locations with the capability of change and transformation.

10.3. At this culmination of the collaborative efforts of countless individuals, the convention podium and steps are barely visible under a roisterous celebration.

10.4. Earliest design concept. Banner-like forms billow in an imagined breeze.

10.5. Requirements for access and visibility begin to shape a speaker's rostrum and locations for photographers and camera operators.

Our design slate ultimately included Margaret Helfand AIA, E. W. Finley PC and Mariano D. Molina Associates (respectively structural and mechanical engineers), and Tom Schwinn, a stage designer. The design group mirrored the cultural diversity of the "Rainbow Coalition" which would assemble in the Garden in July. We needed to demonstrate that we could not only produce a design which could be built within a strict budget and time schedule (these are the words most used as architects and engineers present their credentials at the obligatory interview, the architect's version of the "promise to love, honor and obey"), but, more importantly, that we had a design vision for the setting for this pivotal event. On the basis of a few conceptual sketches illustrating this vision, a record of serious attention to constraints, the combined talents of the collaborative, and the undisguised enthusiasm we had for this unusual undertaking, our team was awarded the commission.

A modern political convention exists on several levels. To the half-dozen candidates and several hundred key insiders, it is a face-to-face conversation, confrontation and accommodation. To the 4,928 Democratic delegates it is a four-day business meeting, political rally, reward for hard work, and chance to party. For the 20,000 commentators, reporters and camera operators, it is a constantly changing spectacle, veering between the humdrum and the dramatic, offering an almost infinite lode to be mined for the sounds and images which can distill nuggets of meaning from the apparent chaos. And, for the millions watching—that visually sated, channel-surfing public inured by countless entreaties to *buy this!*—it is a series of carefully scripted, and sometimes unbelievably spontaneous, images to be pondered (for the relative few ultimately exercising their vote), in making the fateful choice.

The difference between the 1992 national conventions and those of a generation earlier are striking. The mobility of wireless video cameras and microphones make any location a setting for an interview or photo opportunity. The preeminence of television as the medium through which the majority of voters form their opinion of the candidates and issues, coupled with the intense competition for the viewers' attention, make the "look" of the convention setting far more significant than ever before. The granting of the vote to 18-year-olds raised on a diet of several daily hours of TV, and the youth of the leading Democratic candidate, combined to create a convention covered and influenced by MTV.

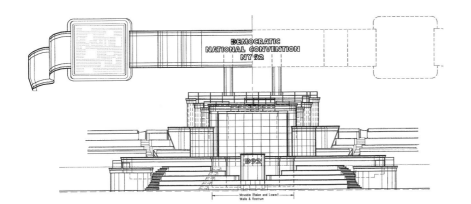

10.6. Elevation: Podium, video-wall backdrop and orchestra platform, and overhead banner were inserted into Madison Square Garden.

The Design Process

The complexity of the event was paralleled by that of the design process, which was to be an extremely intense collaboration involving the individuals already mentioned, members of the various staffs, numerous Federal and City agencies involved with security considerations, and ultimately, a large group of skilled contractors. The DNCC and their advisers determined the message to be communicated by the design. The EDC determined the budget available to realize the design. Network anchorpersons demanded "sky-booths" with unobstructed views as well as unimpeded access to the podium and convention floor. Television and still photographers outlined their requirements for vibration-free camera platforms with superb viewing angles at precise distances from the podium. These vantage points had to be in front of, beside, behind, above, and below the rostrum, so that the candidate could be photographed in every possible relation to the assembled delegates.

The writing press wanted comfortable desks and views of the entire proceedings. The Fire Department demanded wide aisles free of obstruction. The Secret Service sought an environment of perfect security for the "protectee." The state delegations all sought seats of maximum visibility in front of the podium. Each delegation needed telephones and a video console for registering votes. Communications installers required miles of cables under a raised floor. Everybody wanted everything, and right away! While no group got all they wanted, they all got enough of what they needed. Actually, one group, Bill Clinton and Al Gore, did get all they wanted, receiving a boost at the convention which helped carry them to victory.

The design process was a mirror of the convention itself, where a myriad of separate agendas were developed and negotiated until a concept large enough to encompass all would emerge. Like the convention, the design team closeted itself for days on end, emerging only occasionally for food, air and sleep. And, finally merging the design process with the event to come, the final designs were perfected and evaluated on television. A tiny scientific video camera allowed the designers and the various clients to look into the scale models constructed with the same electronic eye which would record the actual event and send it into the homes of millions.

The proof of the power of this design tool was immediate. At the frequent presentations to Democratic Party decision makers, dozens of large drawings and two elaborate models would flank a small television set showing an image picked up by the miniature camera inside one of the models. The attention of our clients seldom wavered from the screen.

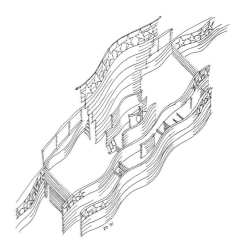

10.7. Various decorative treatments were studied throughout the entire design process.

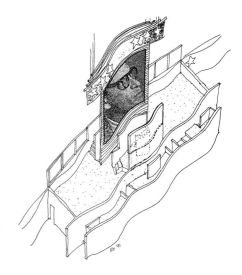

10.8. Early studies for special technical requirements, including video projection, security, access, and ventilation.

10.9. Bold, curved letter forms reinforce the curved platform and steps of the convention podium. *Photo: DNCC.*

Public Place Versus Great Wall

A comparison between the Republican National Convention podium (designed by Robert Keene and held in Houston in August of 1992) and the Democratic podium contrasts two distinctly different design concepts. The Republican podium was surrounded by a high, hard-edged wall separating the candidate from the delegates. (The podium, originally planned to be two feet higher, was lowered in apparent response to the Democratic Convention.) The Democratic podium would be designed as a public plaza linked to the Convention floor by an accessible series of curved steps. It would resemble the *Porta di Ripetta* in Rome, a series of curved steps leading to the Tiber designed in 1703 by Alessandro Specchi, the designer of the more famous Spanish Steps. Like its ancient predecessor, it would be a place of arrival, public gathering and spectacle.

10.10. Republican National Convention podium (designed by Robert Keene) featured straight lines, faceted planes, and a higher platform separated by a wall from the arena floor. *Photo: Courtesy of The White House.*

The Republican podium had an angled rostrum at the edge of the high podium, backed by a tall, right-angled, vertical backdrop further diminishing the apparent scale of any person at the rostrum. The Democratic speakers, in contrast, addressed their audience from a gently curved rostrum at the center of the curved stairs connecting convention floor and podium. At selected moments during the proceedings, the rostrum enclosure, and the flanking wall sections, could be lowered to the level of the podium floor—eliminating completely any physical barrier between candidate and delegate.

10.11. Porta di Ripetta, built in Rome in 1703, was a place of arrival, public gathering and spectacle. From an engraving by Alessandro Specchi. *By permission of George Braziller Publishers.*

The Stanley Elkin quote beginning this section describes such a moment, when the Clinton family arrived at the Garden, walked through the delegates to a tumultuous welcome on the podium steps, and, apparently surprised by the lowering of the rostrum wall, stepped up on the podium. (This "spontaneous" moment was carefully scripted, but the surprise and excitement of those in the Garden was genuine.)

10.12. Static platform becomes a curved screen animated by remotely controlled moving lights, patterns, and colors. (Convention lighting by Immy Fiorentino.) *Photo: DNCC.*

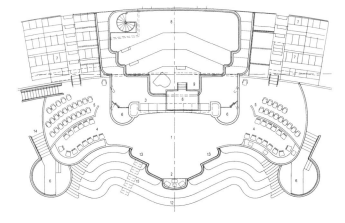

10.13. Floor Plan: Corner turrets flanking both video-wall and platform provide camera locations for still and video coverage.

10.14. The entire undertaking was scaled to respect the dimensions of a single individual standing at the rostrum. *Photo: DNCC.*

The Republican podium was of artificial stone; it tried to project a permanence and solidity that belied its lightweight, ephemeral nature, much as the architecture of Disney World, to which some writers compared it, replicates reality by artifice. The Democratic podium didn't try to imitate something else; the material was neutral and white, a curved screen on which computer-controlled lighting (by Immy Fiorentino, brilliant veteran of many political conventions) superimposed another level of form, pattern, movement, and color. The podium was, at different moments, a background for a variety show, a rostrum, a tiered platform for a chorus or orchestra. At the convention's culminating moment, it was a dance floor. Everything was movement and flux.

The static was further displaced by the dynamic, as the backdrop behind the rostrum, where the speakers and candidates would be filmed, became a video wall of 56 seamlessly joined television screens. This dramatic feature was perhaps the most disturbing aspect of the podium design (and, to a slightly lesser extent, the Republican event, with its two giant video walls flanking the speakers) as the fallible human beings, elected by us to embody our unrealistic expectations of infallibility, address us through the medium of television, dwarfed by their own magnified video images. Television televising television.

Where Do We Go From Here?

It would be disingenuous to criticize a design that I enthusiastically supported. Working on the convention was exciting and fun; the experience of participating with talented professionals from around the country in an event touching the lives of millions was memorable and not to be missed. The design was visually appropriate, functionally effective and representative of the goals of openness and diversity requested by the Democrats. A plasterboard and plywood version of a Baroque piazza had provided a dramatic setting for a public event seen around the world. (This is also appropriate, as the age of the Baroque considered city planning, architecture, and set design equivalent aspects of a single attempt to orchestrate visual harmony and effect.)

A nagging question remains. In a videotape of the 1960 Democratic Convention studied for design precedents, we watched John Kennedy speak, in grainy black and white, from a rostrum not much more elaborate than a card table trimmed in fabric. Although television would already prove crucial in the outcome of that election, there was no video wall, no instant replay, no imposing podium, and little technology to magnify, or diminish, the human being standing before us. The power of a single human voice to move us with its message was unencumbered. Although it doesn't seem possible to go back, which is the more appropriate design?

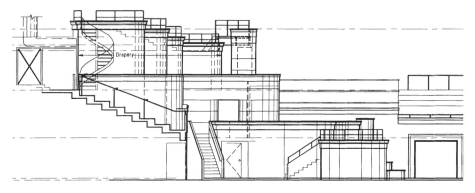

10.15. Elevation: Madison Square Garden arena floor and seating mezzanine supported the temporary, scaffold-supported platform.

10.16. While on the podium they sang "Don't stop thinking about tomorrow," workers in the wings prepared to disassemble the podium. It was gone in a week, with only memories, tape and film remaining. *Photo © NYC Police Department.*

Town & Gown

10.17. Columbia University Stadium. To minimize visual impact, the stadium is partially built into a hillside. Its running track is available for community recreation.

Relations between universities and their neighborhoods have often been less than civil. An attempt by Columbia University in 1968 to locate a gymnasium building in Morningside Park was one of the events triggering the student uprisings of that fateful year. Although the 27-acre Baker Field athletic complex in Upper Manhattan was owned by Columbia, the university was committed to be responsive to community concerns. The design of the new stadium was to respect the spectacular site, minimize the stadium's visual impact on the surrounding residential community, and allow for use of the track during off-hours.

Columbia University

DEDICATION OF THE
LAWRENCE A. WIEN STADIUM AT BAKER FIELD

SEC.

ROW

SEAT

COMMEMORATIVE
TICKET

COLUMBIA
vs.
HARVARD
SAT., SEPT. 22, 1984 — 1:00 PM
RESERVED $6.00

10.18. Architect's original sketch on opening day ticket. Philanthropist Lawrence A. Wien funded this project and many other improvements to New York City communities and institutions.

The wood stadium which was replaced held over 50,000 spectators; the new stadium would seat 10,000, with an additional 5,000 seats in the lower visitors' stands opposite. Keeping the visitors' stands low preserved the views of the Hudson River and New Jersey Palisades from the home stands. The home stand structure is partially on-grade, taking advantage of a natural dip in the site and lessening its effect on adjacent apartment buildings.

10.19. Stadium lower half is cast-in-place concrete on grade. Upper sections (lighter in color) and press box are pre-cast concrete. Central seats are "sold" to donors for fund raising.

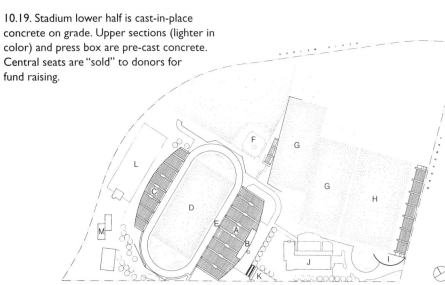

10.20. Site Plan: Stadium, visitors' stands, and running track (left), soccer field and stands (right), practice field (center).
Key:
A   home stand
B   press box
C   proposed visitors stand
D   football field
E   proposed running track
F   baseball field and stand
G   practice fields
H   proposed soccer field and stand
I   proposed maintenance bldg.
J   Christie field house
K   entry gate
L   tennis courts
M   boat house

10.21. Space under stadium houses concession booths, toilets, first-aid facilities and storage.

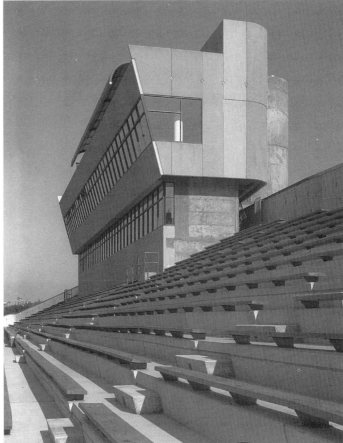

10.22. Level under press box is a VIP Lounge for enclosed viewing and other college events.

10.23. Section: Stadium partly on grade, partly concrete-supported structure. Access to upper levels is by a hydraulic elevator.
Key:
A   press box
B   V.I.P. lounge
C   photographers' shelter
D   elevator tower
E   stadium concourse
F   entry gate
G   V.I.P. seating
H   bench seating
I   track & field

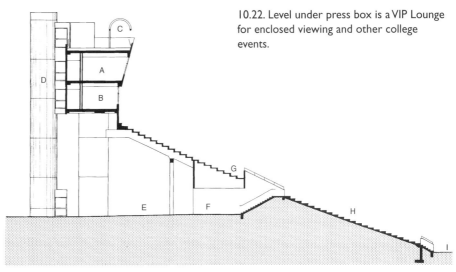

Civil Welcome

10.24. View of Toll Plaza by motorists leaving the United States. The experience of civil departure and leave-taking should be as gracious as that of arrival and welcome. *Rendering: A.C. Bergmann.*

The Rainbow Bridge at Niagara Falls is one of the busiest border crossings into the United States; insufficient toll booths and inadequate U.S. Customs facilities result in massive summer traffic tie-ups. An invited architectural competition sought innovative proposals for ameliorating this national embarrassment. This proposed design demonstrated that a Federal building could be dignified, festive and welcoming without resorting to the formal monumentality characterizing many "official" structures.

10.25. Concept diagram showing a flag-like structure welcoming visitors over the border (see also the DNC 92 concept drawing on p. 202).

Canadian guests are greeted with a friendly wave from a gently undulating building faced in glass-reinforced concrete panels and supported entirely by a double row of structural flagpoles. Flags waving in the border breezes and gently waving walls establish a festive note while the electronic billboard imparts information and fragments of our written heritage to entering and departing visitors. (Thomas Jefferson, designer of the serpentine garden walls at the University of Virginia and a believer in the didactic potential of architecture, might have liked this building.) Have a nice day. Come again real soon.

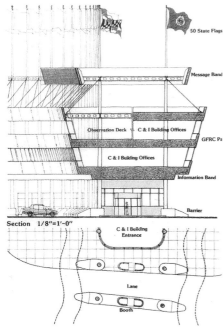

10.26. Section, Part Plan: Building is entirely supported from structural flagpole masts extending to a roof-top observation platform.

10.27. Gently undulating, flag-like facade is suspended from the central columns. Electronic billboard flashing fragments of our written heritage educates visitors and returning citizens waiting at the toll and Customs booths. *Rendering: A.C. Bergmann.*

The Games and After

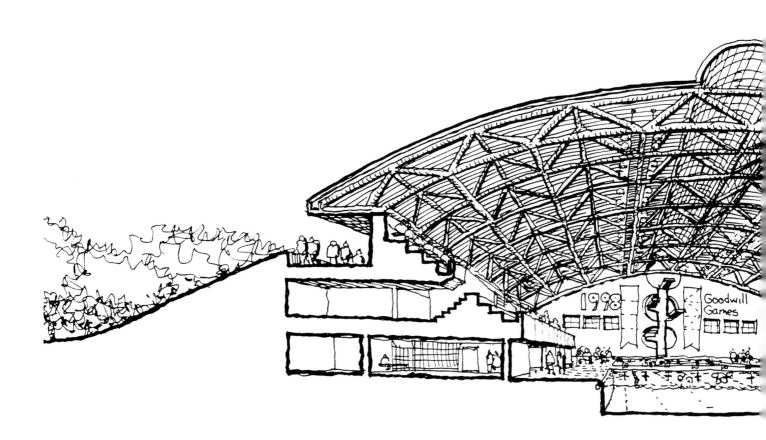

10.28. Aquatic facility is integrated into a natural park by building lockers and permanent seating into an earth berm. Space-frame spans the facility with a gentle arch.

The 1998 Goodwill Games are to be held in the New York Metropolitan region, with the swimming and diving events at a new facility to be built in Nassau County's Eisenhower Park. This selected design deals with two major design issues—locating a large structure in a natural park, and designing a sports facility which can host a world-class event and then revert to a year-round community recreation facility.

The Aquatic Center is a partially earth-sheltered structure utilizing the site's natural contours to fit into a deep swale. Lockers, mechanical spaces and viewing stands are tucked into an earth berm. The south-facing side opens to an outdoor terrace sheltered by the building from north winds. One-half of the 4,500 required spectator seats are in temporary bleachers along this south wall. After the Goodwill Games they will be relocated to a sports area in the park.

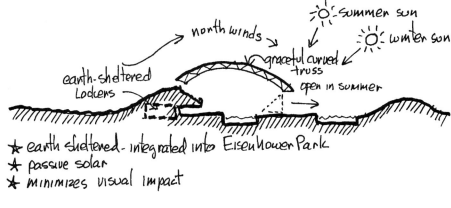

★ earth sheltered - integrated into Eisenhower Park
★ passive solar
★ minimizes visual impact

10.29. Concept diagram: Facility opens to the south, and is earth-sheltered from north winds.

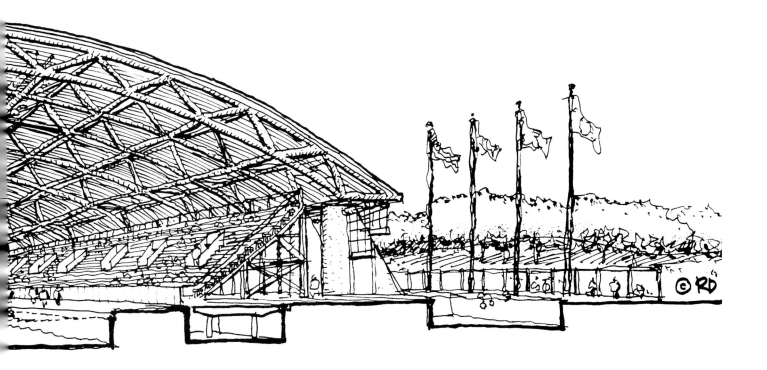

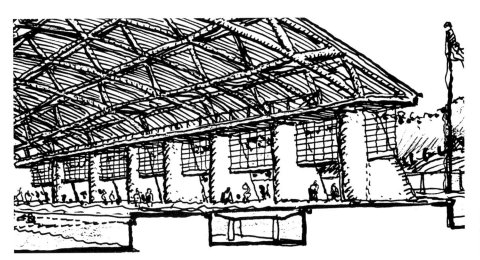

10.30. After the Games are over, temporary bleachers along south wall are relocated, and the pool opened to adjoining outdoor terrace areas.

10.31. Developed scheme with a double-layer
tensile roof suspended from truss arches
spanning between concrete butresses.

10.32. North facade is partially earth-sheltered to allow at-grade entrances to both pool and spectator levels.

10.33. South wall is opened in warm weather to connect indoor pools to outdoor terraces.

Floating Museum

10.34. Lightweight environments constructed on barges are organized around themes of Water, Earth, Atmosphere and Space. Pier 85 anchors the theme park with restaurants and commercial space.

The Intrepid, a preserved World War II aircraft carrier, is permanently moored at Pier 86 in the Hudson River at the foot of West 46th Street in Manhattan. Over the past few years other wartime vessels have been added to this museum of naval warfare and memorial to the men and women who fought at sea. To expand the focus of this waterfront complex, a design was commissioned to develop the adjacent pier as an educational, science-based theme park and museum.

Pier 85 would be developed as a core of restaurants, public boardwalks and commercial space similar to South Street Seaport. Four exhibit barges would be fabricated off-site and towed to a permanent berth at this pier. Exhibition structures on the barges would be organized around themes of Water, Earth, Air and Space.

The exhibits would stress ecological themes and the interrelatedness of these four realms to balance the themes of warfare and destruction so vividly presented on *The Intrepid* and its fleet. The vast human effort, sacrifice and heroism of a nation at war against an evil enemy would serve as a model for a struggle of equal gravity still to come: the struggle to preserve the world.

10.35. New, retractable pedestrian bridge links Pier 85 to the Intrepid Museum at Pier 86.

10.36. Science-based theme park anchors the western end of the 42nd Street tourist corridor, complementing the Intrepid Museum of historic ships and aircraft. Public access to the waterfront is provided around the entire complex. *Rendering: A.C. Bergmann.*

Public Assembly Portfolio

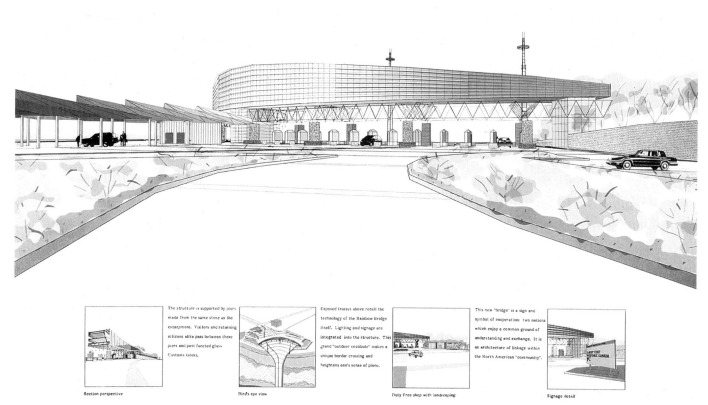

Section perspective

Bird's eye view

Duty Free shop with landscaping

Signage detail

Rainbow Bridge U.S. Plaza, Niagara Falls, New York: *Hardy Holzman Pfeiffer Associates*. The winning entry to this invited competition echoes the Rainbow Bridge with exposed trusses supporting an unbroken arc of translucent glass, which would be "illuminated from behind during the day and floodlit at night. The specially developed glass fractures the natural light into a continually changing rainbow of color and shadow, like the Falls themselves." At this writing, the project is threatened by a publicly organized effort to restore the Falls to a more natural state.

10.37. Faceted glass facade attempts to de-materialize this long arc into a rainbow of colored light changing throughout the day and night. Vehicle inspection shed is at left and duty-free shops at right. *Photo © HHPA*.

NIAGARA FALLS BRIDGE COMMISSION RAINBOW BRIDGE U.S. PLAZA DESIGN COMPETITION

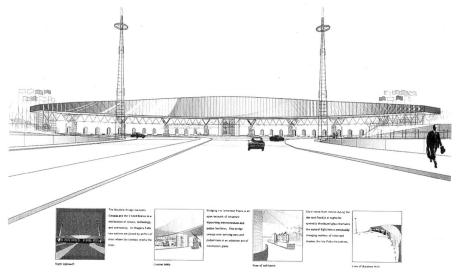

Night approach

Central lobby

View of toll booth

View of Rainbow Wall

ENTRANT 2

10.38. The long arc embraces visitors arriving from Canada.

Virginia Air and Space Center, Hampton, Virginia: *Mitchell/Giurgola, with Rancorn, Wildman, Krause & Brezinski, Architects.* A museum of exploration and discovery in a soaring structure forging a strong, civic link between the waterfront district and the renovated city core.

10.39. View from the water shows the IMAX theater in the white cube under the smaller, arched roof. The taller arched roof shelters a large outdoor plaza at the water's edge. *Photo © Jeff Goldberg/ESTO.*

10.40. The soaring roof is broken into three segments to modulate its size, and a pedestrian-scaled arcade respects the scale of the smaller buildings across the street. *Photo © Jeff Goldberg/ESTO.*

Public Assembly Portfolio

Vietnam Memorial, The Mall, Washington, D.C.: *Maya Lin, Architect.* This is perhaps the most significant work of American civil architecture realized in recent time. It is a triumph of civility and a paradox defying easy categorization. Almost invisible until one comes close, it tears one from the familiar, above-ground surroundings to a kind of temporary resting place below grade. It is at once the most gentle and powerful reminder of the end of all struggle, striving, dying. It is both Ecclesiastes and The Second Law made tangible.

10.41. We are moved by the procession, the deepening wall, the names, the notes, the flowers, those around us sharing the experience. And then, it is the most gentle return to the land of the living above the ground plane. Our complacency is shaken by the descent and we are ennobled by the return. We are, for a time, civilized.
Photo © Maya Lin.

The Future of Civil Architecture

11

Civic Affirmation

An architect of civic facilities comes to see various public buildings as containers for a continuum of human experience, ranging from freedom and self-realization to restraint and a loss of freedom. At the brighter, hopeful pole of this spectrum are the schools, parks, and libraries which facilitate preservation, education, and delight. At the darker, opposite pole are the jails, in which largely unsuccessful efforts are made to rehabilitate the many, and very successful, efforts made to restrain the incorrigible few. In between are the shelters, halfway houses, and "special" schools, in which dedicated staffs attempt to turn their troubled, impaired and unfortunate residents toward the pole of light and hope.

Looking at our society's oscillation between these poles, it is easy to lose hope. The creation of an organization in which freedom and choice can flourish is so much more difficult than tearing it down. The design and construction of a building takes the efforts of hundreds of skilled individuals over a period of years; one sick individual can damage or destroy this building in a few minutes. The effort to educate and socialize a child is immense, in the words of a traditional saying, "It takes a whole village to educate a child." Yet two teen-agers can bring into the world a new person requiring the care of that whole village when they can barely care for themselves, and a child with a gun can erase the life of another in an instant.

The activity of creating architecture is, in its nature, a hopeful act. An architect creates a local, temporary increase in order in a universe of increasing disorder and chaos. In doing so, the architect uses the energy of countless others who likewise wrest from this cooling world the highly organized materials—metal, concrete, glass, lumber, oil—from which a building is assembled. Architect, engineer, builder, client and user share an ancient and noble undertaking. It is, this act of building in the face of eventual dissolution and decay, an act of civic affirmation.

Albert Camus, a survivor of a war-torn Europe, cast one of his alter egos as a physician (in The Plague*) not unlike this writer's view of the architect as physician to society's corpus of the built environment. In his re-casting of* The Myth of Sisyphus *(Alfred A. Knopf, Inc., 1955) Camus comments on Sisyphus, sentenced by the gods to eternally push a rock to the top of a mountain from where it would eternally roll to the bottom.*

"I leave Sisyphus at the foot of the mountain! One always finds one's burden again. But Sisyphus teaches the higher fidelity that negates the gods and raises rocks. He too concludes that all is well. This universe henceforth without a master seems to him neither sterile nor futile. Each atom of that stone, each mineral flake of that night-filled mountain, in itself forms a world. The struggle in itself toward the heights is enough to fill a man's heart. One must imagine Sisyphus happy."

The Future of Civil Architecture

Civility

This book has been about the intertwining of civility and architecture. It has illustrated that civility is an essential attribute of public architecture, and that public architecture is a powerful means for preserving and nurturing both civility and civilization. It might be helpful to examine the current state of civility and architecture separately before hazarding some predictions regarding their linked future.

Charles Dickens' characterization in *The Tale of Two Cities* seems always to describe the present: it is still the best of times and the worst of times. Totalitarian regimes are yielding to free-market economies and increased democracy. Technological advances are increasing the productive capability of the world's economy. At the same time, civility is endangered, beset by uncontrolled population growth, the degradation of our environment and natural resources, the unintended consequences of technology, internecine warfare, ethnic discord, and economic hardship.

If two contemporary cities were nominated to typify the extremes of this dichotomy, Sarajevo, and a similarly tragic Beirut before it, would teach a terrifying lesson in the fragility of civilization. In such settings of chaos and despair, the public realm turns into a killing ground, and architecture reverts to piles of stones separating the hunters from the hunted. When civility dies, architecture dies with it.

Prague, on the other hand, exemplifies the potential for a rebirth of civility and public life after generations of repression. Fortunate to have been spared from the destruction of its historic architecture during both World Wars and the Soviet occupation, Prague had nonetheless seen its public life driven underground. Following the departure of its occupiers, it has flowered into a city of intense cultural activity and public life. One dark cloud on the horizon comes from the recent division of Czechoslovakia into Czech and Slovak ethnic regions.

The forces threatening civility—and the public space and civic architecture which depend on it—are economic as well as political. As the economic structure of Eastern Europe is (or was until very recently) a function of a totalitarian political system, the politics of public life in America are largely a function of our economic system. The past decade has seen an increase in the disparities of income and net worth between rich and poor, employed and unemployed, educated and non-skilled.

In *City of Quartz: Excavating the Future in Los Angeles*, Mike Davis paints an apocalyptic vision of a "Fortress L.A." resembling nothing so much as the metropolis of the film *Blade Runner*. The monied classes confine themselves to super-malls and commercial buildings clustered around sanitized interior spaces, while the poor are relegated to public streets and public parks of diminishing amenities. L.A. police patrol, and impose a harsh order on, a public world inhabited mostly by the unfortunate. Private police guard the fortunate in their protected commercial and shopping centers, and in their fortified, gated residential communities. In Davis' words, "Even as the walls have come down in Eastern Europe, they are being erected all over Los Angeles."

If this bleak vision seems overly without hope, it nonetheless identifies a direction seen in many American communities. The fortunate have retreated from public space, with the resulting impoverishment of that civic realm. Where public parks were once seen as places for different social classes to peacefully coexist, they are increasingly seen as the dangerous precincts of the homeless poor.

The potential result of such a rending of the social fabric is the end of the civic realm as we have known it. Among the most pressing tasks facing our society is the reversal of the polarization threatening our ability to communicate and coexist. Civility and civilization are the necessary prerequisites of public architecture. Ensuring the future of civilization is our main task as social beings and as architects.

Technology vs. Civility

As the automobile dispersed post-war generations into ever-widening circles of suburban, exurban and rural development, we gained mobility at the price of community and civility. The villages, towns, and city neighborhoods which fostered familiarity and community were supplanted by highways, strip commercial development, and malls surrounded by acres of parked cars. The isolation of individuals intensified and civility diminished.

Several recent planning strategies are attempting, with limited success, to restore this lost sense of community and civic life. Recent clustering of higher densities at highway nodes where much of the current growth is taking place (now identified as "edge cities") try to provide the diversity of facilities once found only in central cities. Super-scaled indoor malls enclose hundreds of stores and dozens of restaurants along with amusement rides to keep families occupied, amused, and shopping. Their inherent dependence on the automobile, and their lack of cohesive planning or an organic connection to residential neighborhoods, schools and other civic facilities limit the success of these attempts to replicate *civitas*.

More promising is the movement to develop new communities along lines suggested generations ago by Ebenezer Howard, Clarence Stein, and Henry Wright. The modern versions of these planned neighborhoods and "garden cities" share a pedestrian scale, a clustering around a transit station at the core of the community, and a realization that the automobile must be separated from the pedestrian and tucked out of sight when parked. Two recent books, *The New Community* by Peter Katz, and *Planned Communities* by Peter Calthorpe, ably describe this new/old development.

The problem here is one of economics and equity. These handsomely designed communities are well out of reach of most American families. The few successful communities built on this model (Seaside in Florida is the most familiar example) are single-family, vacation home developments for upper-income residents. Like the beautifully recreated urban memories of the Disney theme parks, these urban experiments risk becoming a flight from a feared civic future, rather than a viable model for our entire society.

The architect's task here is to work for the integration of realistic and practical new development into the fabric of the existing infrastructure and community. The realities of land cost, construction cost, and the cost of building or maintaining roads and utilities suggest denser models (i.e., six-story elevator buildings around courtyards) as a more sensible use of limited resources. The aging of our population and the multiplicity of family work and living arrangements call for a greater variety of flexible housing types, closer to places of work and public transportation. Multi-story apartment structures with fixed utility cores and the capability of converting from small to larger dwelling units by "borrowing" vacant bedrooms from adjacent apartments offer another practical possibility.

The Electronic Future

Just when we thought we had learned enough to plan civil environments dealing intelligently with cars and highways, we find civility and communal life now being challenged by personal computers and the "information superhighway" in ways still not fully understood. Optimists see an electronic link giving everyone instant access to all information, allowing anyone to work anywhere on anything, independent of workplace, commuting, and rush hours. Pessimists posit a nation of isolated workers without benefits or employment security, devoid of face-to-face contact, living day-to-day by their electronic wits. And those are the computer-literate, educated individuals lucky enough to have found employment. Everyone excluded by reason of limited education, lack of access, or other impediment will labor for low wages at menial, dead-end jobs, isolated from the bounty of the digital cornucopia.

The architectural profession is itself in the middle of this technical watershed, both beneficiary and victim of accelerating computerization. While some have gained new powers and capabilities, others have been displaced due to the fewer positions available as architectural practices computerize and "downsize." The only certainty in this tumultuous time is that change will continue to accelerate, and with it, the difficulty of preserving our humanity, compassion, and civility.

Civilian and Warrior

Possibly the most ominous contemporary trend is the blurring of the distinction between the civil and the martial. When there are as many guns as people, when many fear leaving their homes at night, when increasing numbers of us live in enclosed and defended communities, civility and the public architecture to serve it are at risk. Historically, the periods of relative civil peace and freedom which characterize the flowering of civilization are islands in a sea of turmoil and war. Even in our own recent past, nostalgically remembered as a safer, better time, it is important to remember that it was neither safer nor better for those excluded and discriminated against.

The architect's dilemma is here the citizen's dilemma as well. Too much of our architectural history represents a willful disregard for the pain of our fellow citizens while we create environments of beauty and dignity for the privileged few. We can expend our limited efforts to create islands of graciousness in a sea of banality and despair, or use our unique professional talents of vision and organization to create a more modest, but more equitable, setting of utility and dignity for the entire society.

At every moment, civility and chaos, freedom and repression, joy and terror, peace and war, life and death, architecture and rubble, define some of the polarities of human existence and experience. Architecture is the physical manifestation of civility just as rubble is the concrete manifestation of war. Public architecture is an expression of a communal faith in the future.

Architectural Expression

The future form of public architecture will depend to a large extent on the current re-examination of the assumptions on which much of past public architecture was based. It is a debate which also involves public education, religion, multi-culturalism, post-modernism and our shared cultural values.

In *The Saturated Self*, Kenneth J. Gergen argues that new technologies of communication and a multi-cultural society unwilling to agree on a simple definition of truth have supplanted the former dialectic between romanticism (passion, faith, inner-directed values) and modernism (logic, science, rationality). We are left with "post-modernism," a collage of portions of both former positions. The argument goes as follows:

Traditional beliefs formerly held by cohesive cultures are undermined by scientific discovery, inexpensive travel between cultures, and communication technologies allowing for the instant dissemination of a thousand compelling, competing, and conflicting world views. Passionate belief (romanticism) with no objective basis is seen as a dangerous fundamentalist response to the multiplicity of these varied value systems.

At the same time, rationality (modernism) is discredited as the intellectual imperialism of a culturally and economically dominant group (i.e., white males of comfortable means holding positions of institutional power). Scientific findings are similarly suspect as politically biased and further compromised by the inherent limits to knowledge. The two poles therefore call each other into question, canceling each other out as viable options for contemporary man and woman plugged into the bewildering information overload of the electronic highway.

The appropriate response to this multiplicity, argues Gergen, is "post-modernism," a non-committed posture of self-reference, quotation and pastiche. Since both belief and reason are equally discredited, post-modern man and woman are free to provisionally adopt and act out any world view or cultural identity. The Faustian bargain for access to this plethora of styles (literary styles, fashion styles, architecture styles) is the prohibition of either believing in, or claiming a rational basis for, the adopted styles. Everything architectural is possible, from evocations of neo-classical seventeenth-century country villas, to elegant and expensively detailed visions of deconstruction's splintering and chaos. Television advertising and MTV represent post-modernism in its most compelling and ephemeral form.

The Dilemma of Public Architecture

Which qualities are appropriate for the design of civil architecture in a post-industrial society? A post-modern pose appropriate to a fleeting electronic image in the service of selling a product of dubious necessity is not necessarily a valid basis for the design of a public structure which may stand for 70 years (the Biblical three-score years and ten) as an artifact of our shared culture. We need to balance the electronic kaleidoscope of playfully moving colors and images with an anchoring, centering presence of greater *gravity*, in all the varied meanings of that serious word.

The monumentality of past public architecture was largely based on vast scale and the collective effort required to realize it. Ancient Egypt, Imperial Rome, and Haussmann's Paris exemplify civic spaces and structures based on the exercise of absolute political power. The apotheosis of this direction was the plan for central Berlin which Hitler commissioned Albert Speer to design in 1936. For this plan (which, with Speer's memoir,

Inside The Third Reich, should be studied by every architect), Hitler, a failed architect of some talent, and Speer, his most successful architect and alter ego, conceived a civic center of monstrous scale. A boulevard 400 feet wide would pass under a 40-story-high triumphal arch, extending for three miles to a meeting hall where 150,000 people could assemble under a dome 825 feet in diameter. Civic megalomania was to defeat time and mortality, creating an empire which would last 1000 years!

Post-modernism has had a greater success in deflating past pomposity and dogma than in proposing compelling alternatives for the future of architectural expression. One positive lesson of post-modernism is that there is no "true" expression appropriate for civic architecture. Between the Ozymandian illusion of physical immobility and immortality and the present electronic illusion of perpetual motion and novelty, we have to create, for our time, a precarious balance avoiding the excesses and false premises of either extreme.

Ernest Becker showed in *The Denial Of Death* that both of these apparent opposites represent a similar denial of our paradoxical human condition: living beings who know they must die, heroic and pitiful, joyful and tragic, builders and destroyers. We require an intellectual position illustrating F. Scott Fitzgerald's definition of a first-rate intelligence as "the ability to hold two opposed ideas in the mind at the same time, and still retain the ability to function."

Thomas Jefferson, Civic Architect

Thomas Jefferson, our third president, was not only a founder of our nation but its most influential public architect. In an age of political and cultural revolution, he understood that public buildings could embody the permanence and dignity required by the new republic he was helping to create. Jefferson served as Ambassador to France from 1784 to 1789, and was familiar with the work of the great Romantic Classical architects, Boulée and Ledoux.

Beginning with Palladian models, their heroic designs used a bold geometry of sphere, pyramid and cylinder, and aspired to an international and utopian vision expressive of their recent political revolution. Largely unbuilt, these projects called for a vast scale beyond the means of their society. (The grandiosity of their vision would later influence Hitler and his state architect, Albert Speer, in their megalomaniacal fantasies.)

Jefferson's genius was to humanize this architecture to create a uniquely American civic realm, adapting historic precedents to serve a democratic society developing over an apparently limitless landscape. The wildness of nature beyond the eastern seaboard would be civilized by reason and order. Jefferson was instrumental in superimposing a Cartesian grid of survey lines over both the new city of Washington, D.C., and the territories beyond.

Yes, I know. The imposition of one man's (or woman's, or culture's) order is invariably at someone else's expense. Jefferson's reason and order ultimately supplanted native civilizations which had long had a more balanced symbiosis with this land. Any action or speech immediately calls itself into question as endlessly conflicting views test each other, like mirrors endlessly reflecting. Balance is everything.

Faced by civil unrest, poverty, racial violence, political discord, and threats from abroad (some things don't change!), the new republic nonetheless required public buildings commensurate with its hopes. In what many consider his greatest work, the University of Virginia, Jefferson managed that tightrope walk required by a civil architecture, a balance between human scale and monumentality, order and openness, aspirations and means, building and landscape, permanence and change.

Criteria for Civil Architecture

In the knowledge that there are no absolute truths, that all is provisional and subject to the very human limits of our (my) imagination, let me postulate some design criteria for a Civil Architecture appropriate to the troubled and promising near future of our wonderful, vulnerable planet. These design goals aim at a public architecture which might help mend some of the tears in our shared social fabric, express the interdependence of our civic life, and embody our aspirations for a communal future. Jefferson's University of Virginia serves to illustrate many of these:

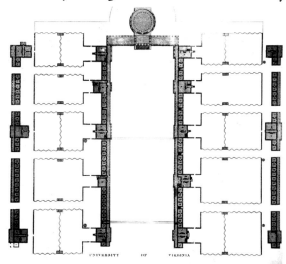

11.1. Jefferson's plan for the University of Virginia. An "academical village" around a central lawn. Student dwellings and a loggia link ten professors' houses illustrating ten architectural orders. The Rotunda completes this wonderful composition. *Photo: University of Virginia Library.*

A Modest Monumentality

Even as excessive monumentality can extinguish humanity, insufficient scale undermines the sense of permanence and communal memory suitable for a civic structure. Jefferson's Rotunda at the University of Virginia was based on the Roman Pantheon, but at half-scale. The result transformed a vast temple of worship into a modestly imposing place of learning. The tension between the need to express the significance of civic facilities and the desire to create humane, accessible settings for public life is perhaps the most difficult balance for an architect to achieve.

The Nobility of Aspiration

Jefferson saw this campus as "an academical village," a community of professors and students united in their striving for learning and practical truths. In Jefferson's time the nobility of this public undertaking supplanted the nobility of the recently overthrown royal court. For our time, the nobility of our society's aspirations to preserve and enhance public life can bridge some of the faults created as cultures clash. An aspiration to democratic goals, seriousness of purpose, and the dignity of human effort characterized Jefferson's work. They are no less suitable for today's equally beleaguered civilization.

Sustainability

An economy of means, doing more with less, was as central to Jefferson the Inventor as to our own time's Buckminster Fuller. Conserving material, human and natural resources was essential to a fledgling nation and remains so today. Public architecture must set a special example by being efficiently built, long-lasting, and energy-conserving. The recent movement toward sustainability in architecture is a welcome development.

Contextuality

French public buildings of Jefferson's time generally dominated the natural landscape, imposing a man-made geometry expressive of political control over nature's topography. The native villages and early Colonial settlements of the new republic were generally modestly scaled and dominated by their surroundings. At the University of Virginia, Jefferson merged building, garden, and nature in a wonderful balance, neither dominating, nor dominated by the surrounding landscape.

11.2. The "lawn" at the University of Virginia. Jefferson balanced architecture and nature in a setting of appropriate scale and unsurpassed civility.

Inclusiveness and Accessibility

Jefferson's campus housed professors and students in quarters linked by a unifying colonnade. Although the professors' houses are grander than the students' residences, both are accommodated within this academical village embracing a terraced village green. The Rotunda presides over this gentle ensemble; its fourth wall was originally the natural landscape beyond. All were included: teacher and pupil, enclosure and void, man and nature. Physical inclusiveness and accessibility is now the law of the land. Future civil architecture will need to build from this requirement a higher level of accessibility, where all are included, valued, and welcomed.

An Acceptance of Contradiction

Jefferson's new republic, like our own evolving society, was continuously creating itself out of, and in contradiction to, its social, political, and cultural precursors. Poised between the rejection of a familiar past and the unknown future, between tradition and innovation, Jefferson improvised. He was not reluctant to adapt historic architectural forms to better serve the novel social institutions the new nation would require. Previous eras had the luxury of an accepted style for public architecture. Our situation, like Jefferson's, is more interesting, and therefore more challenging. (The ancient Chinese saying, "You should live in interesting times!" is a curse, not a benediction.) The passing of Absolute Truth can allow a myriad of provisional truths to flower. A multi-cultural society can withstand multiple interpretations of appropriateness for civic structures.

An Architecture Which Educates

Jefferson intended the 10 professors' houses to teach, by their example, 10 lessons about architecture and history. Winston Churchill recognized the didactic dimension of architecture in his statement that "we make our buildings, and then they make us." The public architecture of the WPA ennobled its society in buildings, murals, and sculpture. Architecture can reveal its construction, teach about mechanical systems, and make visible the activities within. A civil architecture for our time can also teach about mutuality, regional diversity, sustainability, and the heroism of daily life.

Civility (All of the Above)

Jefferson and his peers attempted a society based on respect for the individual. The basis of a civil architecture is the same concern. Buildings, like individuals, have voices. Jefferson's respect for reason and order was made tangible in a public architecture approximating a conversation among equals, with every voice both respecting and respected. A building is in a conversation with its users and surroundings, responding to their needs in a dialogue of sensitivity and respect. The alternative—in both public discourse and public architecture—is the experience of a noisy restaurant, the modern equivalent of "the tragedy of the commons." In order to be heard, everyone's voice is gradually raised, and in the increasing cacophony no one can finally be understood. In too much of our shared existence, volume is the enemy of meaning.

In a civil conversation, all the variety of human imagination and aspiration can be heard. A civil architecture ultimately aims to house, protect, nurture, and ennoble this discourse of civilization. In a world of endless wonder, where certainty is ever doubted, we can sustain in conversation a circle of approximate truths surrounding a mystery.

Bibliography

Atkins, P. W. *The Second Law.* New York, NY: W. H. Freeman & Co., 1984.
A beautiful, cogent presentation of the Second Law of Thermodynamics. Understanding of this law should be a requirement for holding public office, obtaining a driver's license, becoming a citizen.

Becher, Bernd & Hilla. *Blast Furnaces.* Cambridge: MIT Press, 1990.
Pick up this beautiful book depicting blast furnaces from around the world and select any page. The frontal, black and white photographs are all the same (same angle, same cloudy light) and are all different. To study one photograph for ten minutes is to understand something of the heroism and nobility of vast human constructions. These works of architecture rival the cathedrals. The Bechers have also documented mine heads, water tanks, and gas tanks.

Becker, Ernest. *The Denial of Death.* New York: The Free Press, 1973.
An Ecclesiastes *for modern times, one of those few books that illuminate human existence. The lesson for architects is still "vanity, vanity, all is vanity, and striving after wind."*

Betsky, Aaron. "Tearing Down The Temple: The New Civic Architecture." New York: *Architectural Record,* October 1993.

Calthorpe, Peter. *The Next American Metropolis: Ecology, Community and the American Dream.* New York: Princeton Architectural Press, 1994.

Caudill, William W. *Toward Better School Design.* New York: F. W. Dodge Corporation, 1954.

Cohen, Peter. *The Architecture of Doom.* Berlin: c. 1991.
This documentary film made from Nazi archives illustrates civil architecture gone mad. The scale of the stadiums, parade grounds, and assembly buildings planned by Hitler's architect (Albert Speer) would have surpassed civic constructions built by any civilization.

Cutler, Phoebe. *The Public Landscape of the New Deal.* New Haven: Yale University Press, 1985.
A study of the effect of the construction programs of the Roosevelt years on parks, parkways, and the profession of Landscape Architecture.

Dattner, Richard. *Design for Play.* New York: Van Nostrand/Reinhold, 1969.

Genevro, Rosalie. *New Schools for New York:* New York: Princeton Architectural Press, 1992.
This work grows out of a study and architectural competition sponsored by the Architectural League of New York and the Public Education Association. It contains a concise summary of public school design in New York City, as well as numerous competition entries for small schools on a number of actual sites.

Gergen, Kenneth J. *The Saturated Self: Dilemmas Of Identity In Contemporary Life.* New York: Basic Books, 1991.

Gillon, Edmund V., Jr. *Pictorial Archive of Early Illustrations and Views of American Architecture.* Mineola, NY: Dover Publications Inc., 1971.

Glazer, Nathan. *The Public Face of Architecture.* New York: Free Press, 1987.

Graebner, William. *Coming Of Age In Buffalo.* Philadelphia: Temple University Press, 1990.

Graves, Ben E. *School Ways: The Planning and Design of America's Schools.* New York: McGraw-Hill, Inc., 1993.
A compendium of recent school architecture, by the former director of the Ford Foundation's Educational Facilities Laboratories—a now defunct "think tank" for the design of schools which had, in its time, an immense impact on public architecture.

Gray, Christopher. *Changing New York: The Architectural Scene.* Mineola, NY: Dover Publications Inc., 1992.

Hoyt, Charles King. *Public, Municipal, and Community Buildings*. New York: McGraw-Hill, 1980.

Huxtable, Ada Louise. "Inventing American Reality." *The New York Review:* December 3, 1992.

Katz, Peter. *The New Urbanism: Toward An Architecture Of Community*. New York: McGraw-Hill, Inc., 1994.

Klinkenborg, Verlyn. *The Last Fine Time*. New York: Alfred A. Knopf, Inc., 1990.
A weaving together of place (Buffalo NY), time (1947), and the author's in-laws in a prose poem of the everyday and ordinary. A hauntingly beautiful depiction of the end of an era in an American city built on heavy industry and the sweat of immigrants.

Mahar-Keplinger, Lisa. *Grain Elevators*. New York: Princeton Architectural Press, 1993.
Le Corbusier, Eric Mendelsohn, Charles Sheeler, Dorothea Lange (and a young Richard Dattner)—all were fascinated by these Midwest cathedrals built to store grain. The author presents a handsome typology of these structures in wood, steel, and concrete.

Muschamp, Herbert. Various Architecture Articles. *The New York Times*, 1992–1994.

Roth, Leland. *McKim, Mead & White 1879–1915*. New York: Benjamin Blom (1973), Arno Press (1977), 1915, 1973, 1977.

Schonhaut, Charles et al. *Middle School Task Force Report*. New York: New York City Board of Education, 1988.
A study recommending that the population of middle (intermediate) schools be limited to about 600 students— to create a community where students would be known by name to teachers and school administration.

Short, C. W. *Survey of the Architecture of the Public Works Administration*. Washington, D.C.: PWA, 1940.

Solzhenitsyn, Aleksandr. "The Relentless Cult of Novelty And How It Wrecked the Century." *New York Times Book Review*, February 7, 1993.

Speer, Albert. *Inside The Third Reich*. New York: The Macmillan Company, 1970.
Hitler and Speer left the realm of civilization, creating a demonic landscape which attempted to crush by its grandiosity all human fallibility and mortality. A cautionary tale for architects and other humans.

White, Norval and Willensky, Elliot. *AIA Guide to New York City*. New York: Harcourt Brace Jovanovich, 1988.

Acknowledgments & Credits

Project Credits

Architects of projects in the Portfolio Sections are identified in the captions, as are photographers and/or archival sources for photos throughout the book. Projects not otherwise identified are by Richard Dattner Architect P.C. Photographs and drawings not otherwise identified are by Richard Dattner. The following projects are listed by chapter, with associated architects and engineers where applicable:

Chapter 1: McCarren Park Play Center (Proposal): Owner: NYC Parks Department, *Richard Dattner Architect.* **Asphalt Green AquaCenter:** Owner: NYC Parks Department. Operating Entity: Asphalt Green Inc. *Richard Dattner Architect; Goldreich Page & Thropp Structural Engineer; Caretsky Associates Mechanical Engineer; Abel Bainnson Butz Landscape Architect; Counsilman Hunsaker Pool Consultant.* **Louis Armstrong Cultural Center:** Owner: NYC Department of General Services. Operating Entity: ELMCOR. *Richard Dattner Architect; Goldreich Page & Thropp Structural Engineer; Herbert Kunstadt Mechanical Engineer; Abel Bainnson Butz Landscape Architect; Artist: Howard McCalebb.* **Bellevue-Rusk Rehabilitation Park:** Owner: Bellevue Hospital. *Richard Dattner Architect.* **Tampa Riverfront Park:** Owner: City of Tampa. *Richard Dattner Architect; Goldreich Page & Thropp Structural Engineer; Harold Hecht Mechanical Engineer; Vreeland & Guerriero Landscape Architect.* **Thomas Jefferson Pool Center:** Owner: NYC Parks Department. *Richard Dattner Architect; Goldreich Page & Thropp Structural Engineer; Wesler & Cohen Mechanical Engineer; Miceli Kulik Williams Landscape Architect.*

Chapter 2: Riverbank State Park: Owner: New York State Office of Parks, Recreation & Historic Preservation. Construction Agency: New York State Office of General Services. *Richard Dattner Architect; Abel Bainnson Butz Landscape Architect; E.W. Finley Structural Engineer; Daniels Barnes Wesler & Cohen Mechanical Engineers.*

Chapter 3: I.S. 218: Owner: NYC Board of Education. Construction Agency: NYC School Construction Authority. *Richard Dattner Architect; Goldreich Page & Thropp Structural Engineer; Robert Derector Mechanical Engineer; Miceli Kulik Williams Landscape Architect; Artists: Joyce Kozloff, Pat Steir.* **I.S. 2 Brooklyn, I.S. 5 Queens, I.S. 90 Manhattan, I.S. 171 Brooklyn:** Owner: NYC Board of Education. Construction Agency: NYC School Construction Authority. *Richard Dattner Architect; Goldreich Page & Thropp (I.S. 2, I.S. 5, I.S. 90) and Ysrael A. Seinuk (I.S. 171) Structural Engineer; KFA (I.S. 2, I.S. 90), KFA/DVL (I.S. 5), and Mariano D. Molina (I.S. 171) Mechanical Engineer; Miceli Kulik Williams (I.S. 2, I.S. 5, I.S. 90) Blumberg & Butter (I.S. 171) Landscape Architect; Artists: Emma Amos, Ronald Baron, Donna Dennis, Kate Ericson & Mel Zeigler, Sung Ho Choi, Roberto Juarez, Jacqueline Lima, Ed Rath, David Saunders, Martin Wong.* **Maxwell High School:** Owner: NYC Board of Education. Construction Agency: NYC School Construction Authority. *Richard Dattner Architect; Ysrael A. Seinuk Structural Engineer; Mariano D. Molina Mechanical Engineer; Blumberg & Butter Landscape Architect.* **P.S. 11 Queens, P.S. 128 Manhattan:** Owner: NYC Board of Education. Construction Agency: NYC School Construction Authority. *Richard Dattner Architect; Goldreich Page & Thropp Structural Engineer; KFA Mechanical Engineer; Abel Bainnson Butz Landscape Architect.* **Beginning With Children School:** Owner: NYC Board of Education. Operating Entity: Beginning With Children Inc. *Richard Dattner Architect (Phase 1), Prentice & Chan, Ohlhausen (Phase 2); Ysrael A. Seinuk Structural Engineer; Mariano D. Molina Mechanical Engineer.* **P.S. 380:** Owner: NYC Board Of Education. *Richard Dattner Architect; Goldreich Page & Thropp Structural Engineer; Wald & Zigas Mechanical Engineer; A.E. Bye Landscape Architect; Artist: Knox Martin.*

Chapter 4: P.S. 234: Owner: NYC Board of Education. *Richard Dattner Architect; Goldreich Page & Thropp Structural Engineer; Robert Derector Mechanical Engineer; Miceli Kulik Williams Landscape Architect; Artist: Donna Dennis.*

Chapter 5: Townsend Harris Hall, CCNY: Owner: City University of New York. Construction Agency: Dormitory Authority of the State of New York. *Richard Dattner Architect; Goldreich Page & Thropp Structural Engineer; Robert Derector Mechanical Engineer.* **CUNY Law School Legal Clinic:** Owner: City University of New York. Construction Agency: Dormitory Authority of the State of New York. *Richard Dattner Architect; Goldreich Page & Thropp Structural Engineer; Robert Derector Mechanical Engineer.* **Brooklyn College Dining Facility:** Owner: City University of New York. *Richard Dattner Architect; Goldreich Page & Thropp Structural Engineer; Robert Derector Mechanical Engineer.* **Parkchester Branch Library:** Owner: New York Public Library. Construction Agency: NYC Department of General Services. *Richard Dattner Architect; Goldreich Page & Thropp Structural Engineer; Robert Derector Mechanical Engineer; Artist: Marcia Dalby.*

Chapter 6: Sludge Dewatering Facilities, Sludge Storage Facilities: Owner: NYC Department of Environmental Protection. *Stone & Webster/Hazen & Sawyer - Joint Venture Engineers; Richard Dattner Design Architect; Abel Bainnson Butz Landscape Architect.* **W. 59th Street and W. 135th Street Marine Transfer Stations:** Owner: NYC Department of Sanitation. *Greeley & Hansen Engineers; Richard Dattner Design Architect; Artist: Steven Antonakos.* **Greenpoint Marine Transfer Station:** Owner: NYC Department of Sanitation. *EBASCO Engineers; Richard Dattner Design Architect.*

Chapter 7: Sherman Creek State Park: Owner: New York State Office of Parks, Recreation & Historic Preservation. *Richard Dattner Architect; Robert Rosenwasser Structural Engineer; Hecht, Hartmann & Concessi Mechanical Engineer; Steven Olko Marine Engineer.* **Con Edison Customer Service Facility, "The Hub":** Owner: Consolidated Edison. *Richard Dattner Architect; Robert Rosenwasser Structural Engineer; KFA Mechanical Engineer; Abel Bainnson Butz Landscape Architect.* **Con Edison Customer Service Facility, Westchester Square:** Owner: Consolidated Edison. *Richard Dattner Architect; Goldreich Page & Thropp Structural Engineer; Aaron Zicherman Mechanical Engineer; Vreeland & Guerriero Landscape Architect.*

Chapter 8: Ridge Street Gardens, Clinton Gardens: Owner: New York Foundation for Senior Citizens. Funding Agency: U.S. Housing and Urban Development 202 Program. *Richard Dattner Architect; Rosenwasser Grossman Structural Engineer; I.M. Robbins Mechanical Engineer; Abel Bainnson Butz Landscape Architect.* **Leake & Watts Children's Home:** Owner: Leake & Watts. Funding Agency: Dormitory Authority of the State of New York. *Richard Dattner Architect; Carlo Zaskorski Associated Architect; Ysrael A. Seinuk Structural Engineer; Mariano D. Molina Mechanical Engineer; Quennell & Rothschild Landscape Architect.* **Riverside Park Community/I.S. 195:** Construction Agency: NYC Housing, Preservation and Development and NYC Board of Education. *Richard Dattner Architect; Max Wechsler, Henri LeGendre Associated Architects; Robert Rosenwasser Structural Engineer; Scherr Kopelman Mechanical Engineer; Coffey Levine & Blumberg Landscape Architect.*

Chapter 9: NYC Police Academy (2nd Prize Competition Entry): Owner: NYC Police Department. Construction Agency: NYC Department of General Services. *Richard Dattner Architect; Ysrael A. Seinuk Structural Engineer; Mariano D. Molina Mechanical Engineer; Abel Bainnson Butz Landscape Architect.* **NYC Youth Center (Proposal):** Owner: NYC Juvenile Justice. Construction Agency: NYC Department of General Services. *Richard Dattner Architect.*

Chapter 10: Democratic National Convention 1992: Construction Agency: NYC Economic Development Corporation. *Richard Dattner Architect; Margaret Helfand Associated Architect; Tom Schwinn Stage Design; Immy Fiorentino Lighting Design; E.W. Finley Structural Engineer; Mariano D. Molina Mechanical Engineer; Service Station Graphics.* For the Democratic Convention Coordinating Committee: *Gary Smith Production, Rene Lagler Stage Design.* **Columbia University Stadium:** Owner: Columbia University. *Richard Dattner Architect; Geiger-Berger Structural Engineer; Wesler Cohen Mechanical Engineer.* **Rainbow Bridge Toll Plaza (Invited Competition):** *Richard Dattner Architect.* **1998 Goodwill Games Aquatic Center:** Owner: NYS Urban Development Corporation. Construction Agency: NYS Dormitory Authority. Operating Agencies: Goodwill Games Organizing Committee, Nassau County. *Richard Dattner Architect; Severud Associates Structural Engineer; Counsilman Hunsaker Pool Consultant; Abel Bainnson Butz Landscape Architect.* **Intrepid Park:** Owner: The Intrepid Museum. *Richard Dattner Architect.*

Acknowledgments

The following organizations and individuals are acknowledged for their contributions to the illustrated projects:

Asphalt Green AquaCenter: *Albert & Barrie Zesiger, Frank Angelino, Leslie Herrmann, Raquel Ramati, Jan Ryan, Jack Scaldini, Carol Tweedy, Howard Weiss.*

Beginning With Children School: *Carol and Joseph Reich, Bruce Barrett, Anthony Carcich, Tom Kline, Michael Trocchio.*

Bellevue-Rusk Rehabilitation Park: *Connie Solomon, Joanne Veit.*

Con Edison Facilities: *Richard Ball, Mitch Benerofe, Leon Brand, Bill Mezzabarba, Frank Sciame, Allen Scudder, Joseph Tomei.*

1998 Goodwill Games Aquatic Center: *Robert Johnson, Don Smith, Matt Scheckner, Steve Chriss, Mary-Jean Eastman.*

Greenpoint MTS: *K. Ilachinsky.*

Leake & Watts Children's Home: *Margery Ames, Paul Barnes, James Campbell, Dennis Castro, Harold Gabriel, Peter Nesbitt, David Schunter, David Todd, Charlie Winter.*

Louis Armstrong Cultural Center: *Jeffrion Aubrey, Cecil Watkins, Elwanda Young.*

Nassau County: *John Kiernan, Kevin Ocker, John Waltz*

P.S. 234: *Blossom Gelertner, Anna Switzer, Amy Heinrich, Emmy Devine, Kathryn Freed, Paul Goldstein.*

Ridge Street and Clinton Gardens: *Linda Hoffman, Zibby Tozer, Bob Borg, Pete Cettina, John Cricco, Reuben Glick, Jerry Hirschen, Pat Kelly, Jane Mallow, John Nowak, Esther Ranz, Joan Ulbrich, Joseph Zelazny.*

Riverside Park Community: *Dan Gray, John Johnson, Joseph Overton, Bernie Spiess.*

Sludge Dewatering Facilities: *Mike Hartmann, George Marinos.*

Tampa Riverfront Park: *Joel Jackson, Ron Rotella, Rick Smith.*

The following public agencies and individuals are acknowledged for their support and participation in one or more of the projects illustrated. As it takes an entire village to educate one child, hundreds of persons are required to realize one work of civic architecture. This list includes some of those who added their efforts to the realization of the work shown.

Bronx Borough President: *Hon. Fernando Ferrer.*

Brooklyn Borough President: *Hon. Howard Golden, Greg Brooks.*

Brooklyn College/CUNY: *Steve Czirak, Rose Erwin, Bill Farrell, Robert Hess, Walter Litvak.*

Brooklyn Public Library: *Frank DiRosa, Helmut Hutter.*

City College of New York/CUNY: *Joan Hill.*

City University of New York: *Norman Becker, Robert Buxbaum, Dana Colban, Corwin Frost, John Hanson, Arthur Rubenstein.*

Manhattan Borough President: *Hon. Ruth Messinger, Hon. Percy Sutton.*

NYC Art Commission: *Ed Ames, Flora Miller Biddle, Lo-yi Chan, Jim Freed, Brad Greene, Patricia Harris, Lauren Otis, Robert Ryman, John T. Sargant, Nanette Smith, Anita Soto, Vivian Millicent Warfield, John Willenbecher, E. Thomas William, Jr.*

NYC Board of Education: *Chancellors Joseph Fernandez & Ramon Cortines, Jay Ames, Michele Cohen, Ralph Dimartino, Greg Frux, Kathy Gallo, August Gold, Amy Linden, Monroe Nadel, Joseph Nappi, Arthur Panetta, Marion Pasnik.*

NYC Council: *Councilmen Guillermo Linares and Stanley Michels.*

NYC Dept. of Cultural Affairs: *Commissioner Schuyler G. Chapin, Tom Finkelpearl, Jennifer McGregor, Janet Oliver.*

NYC Dept. of Environmental Protection: *Commissioner Marilyn Gelber, Robert Adamski, Mike Cetera, Nick Ilijic, Robert Lemieux, Christian Meyer, Glen Vogel.*

NYC Dept. of General Services: *Commissioner William Diamond, Richard Banks, Adrienne Bresnan, Robert Boyars, Hillary Brown, John Campbell, Steve DiStefano, David Eng, Ivan Ilyashov, Herbert Jaslow, Anne Khoury, Phil Killwey, Herbert Lackner, Sang Lee, Jerry Maltz, Tony Smith, James Trent, Thomas Vanacore, Mario Villalobos, Sarelle Weisberg.*

NYC Dept. of Housing Preservation & Development: *Peter Brady, Arlene Gamza, Steve Faicco, Jeff Jacobsen, Charles Pumilia, Herbert Siegel.*

NYC Dept. of Parks & Recreation: *Commissioners Henry Stern, Betsy Gotbaum, and Tom Hoving, Luis Aragon, Jonathan Kuhn, Fred Little, Charles McKinney, Alan Moss, George Olsen, Patrick Pompasello, Steve Rosenthal, Ed Schubert, Richard Schwartz, Adrian Smith, Paul Stanton, Kuo Ming Tsu, Stephen Whitehouse.*

NYC Dept. of Sanitation: *Paul Casowitz, Mike Friedlander, Jacob Holchendler, Anthony Zarillo.*

NYC Economic Development Corp.: *Hardy Adasko, Clay Lifflander, James Schmidt, Jonathan Winer, Margot Woolley.*

NYC Housing Authority: *Robert Biviano, Glenn Brown, David Burney, Anthony Filippini, Ilwon Kang, Nancy Osteicher, Eftihia Tsitiridis.*

NYC School Construction Authority: *Chairman Donal E. Farley, Founding Trustee Meyer S. Frucher, President & CEO Barry Light, Louis Auricchio, Earl Brown, Ash Chakraborty, Cindy Dial, Rose Diamond, Sal Federico, Azita Ganji, Maureen Grinnan, Russell Imbrenda, Bob Jefferson, Stanley Kalb, Mike Kaleda, Ken Karpel, Stuart Kitain, Robert Landrigan, Joseph Lucaselli, Arlene Malone, Dan Millman, Peter Naas, Prakash Nair, Charles Ng, Stan Petrow, Tom Spiers, Deborah Taylor, Fitz Wilson, Steve Woodchecke, Al Venturini.*

NYC Office of Mayor: *Mayor Rudolph Guiliani, former Mayors John Lindsay, Ed Koch & David Dinkins, Deputy Mayors Barbara Fife & Robert Esnard.*

NYC Transit Authority: *Jeff Anschlowar, Valery Baker, Sandra Bloodworth, T. J. Costello, Wendy Feuer, Larry Krasnoff, Vijay Sawant, John Tarantino.*

NYS Assembly: *Representatives Herman Farrell and Brian Murtaugh.*

NYS Dormitory Authority: *Commissioner Rudolph Rinaldi, Vin Barone, Raymond Barsa, Michael Creegan, Walter Kelly, Peter McGlinchey, Robert McLaughlin, Frank Vinci, Douglas Van Vleck.*

NYS Office of General Services: *Commissioners John Egan and Ray Casey, Burdeen Hanson, Robert Levin, Jim Panagopoulos, Robert Santoro, David Sieffert, Richard Thomas, Pete Vezos, Paul Waterson.*

NYS Office of Mental Health: *Cindy Friedmutter, Sally Greene, Lorena Robinson-Saeed, Mona Roth, Ana Topolevec.*

NYS Office of Parks, Recreation & Historic Preservation: *Commissioners Orin Lehman & Joan Davidson, Hector Aponte, John Bagley, Claire Beckhardt, Albert Caccese, Anne Fahim, Elizabeth Goldstein, Warren Holliday, Dan Maciejak, Gaspar Santiago, Ivan Vamos.*

NYS Senate: *Senator Franz Leichter.*

NYS Urban Development Corp.: *Vincent Tese, Robert Brugger, Frances Huppert, Arpad Klausz, Paul Slusarev, Jacqueline Wright.*

Port Authority of NY & NJ: *Martin Appel, elyse bankler, Demo Christaforatos, Juan Cortes, Robert Davidson, Gil Dillon, Gene Fasullo, Richard Franklin, Martin Hero, Paul Hollick, John Keyser, Karen Lombardo, Conrad Schaub.*

Queens Borough President: *Hon. Claire Schulman, Peter Magnani, Mike Sinansky.*

US Department of Housing & Urban Development: *Robert Basolino, Alfredo Fredericks, Beryl Nywood, Peggy Sheehan, Richard Woods.*

The architects, architects-in-training, draftspersons and administrative staff listed below participated in our civil efforts over the past 30 years. The work illustrated, and this book, would not have existed without their contributions:

Craig Abel, Jennifer Adler, James Anderson, Helen Angeles, Terry Bailey, Paul Bauer, Amy Benenson, Walter Broner, Claribel Byer, Mark Camera, Felicia Campanella, Rick Carpenter, Ted Ceraldi, Songsri Chang, Sandra Chase, David Cipperman, Harvey Cohn, Joseph Coppola AIA, Kevin Daken, Keith Daniels, Michael Daniels, Gerald Davis, Robert Drake, Merle Deen, Stefanos Eapen, Susan Ecker, Dan Erez, Philippe Erville, Michael Esposito, David Falk,

Crystal Felder, Diego Feraru, Mimi Florance, Jenny French, Evelyn Gamez, Haritini Geiser, Mark Ginsberg AIA, Beth Greenberg AIA, Pat Guadagno, Barry Goldsmith, Carolyn Hunter, Daniel Heuberger, Jonathan Jaffe, Rowena Kabigting, Barbara Kalish, Michelle Kayon, Jeffry Keiffer, William Kelm, Laura Kiaulenas, Jonathan Klausz, Randy Korman, Carolinn Kuebler, Boris Lakhman, John Lam AIA, Betsy Lanier, Naomi Leiseroff, Michael Lenahan, Gloria Lim, Judy Lowenthal, Jeffrey Luy, David Mann, Katrina Maxino, Mike Mayo, Deborah McManus, Deanna C. Medina, Richard Metzner, Henry Meltzer, Evelyn Menendez, Victor Migneco, Daniel Mitchell, Monty Mitchell, Bernardo Ngui, Deborah Norden, Michael Notaro, Jaime Ortega AIA, Mathew Park, Nora Pieter, Tony Pileggi, Frank Prial, Jr., Hernando Quijano, Ramon Quiray, Channing Redford, John Reistetter, John Roundtree, Lydia Ruiz, David Sacks, Carlos Sainz, Steve Secon, Fariba Shirdel, Kenneth Shook AIA, Ellen Shoskes, Frances Soliven, Peter Sprung, Michael Stein, William Stein AIA, Henrietta Susser, Donna Taraschuk, Marge Thomas, Henry Thompson, Omolade Jacob Tukuru, Solita Wakefield, Linda Walker, Angela Wheeler, Roger Whitehouse, Allan Willig, Susan Woo, Bernard Zipprich AIA, Bernie Zalon.

Rachelle Dattner gave me the benefit of her careful reading of the text and many important suggestions. Benjamin and Laura Dattner read portions of the text and contributed the viewpoint of a younger generation.

Special thanks go to Vilma Barr for her valuable assistance during the book's early stages and her careful and intelligent editing. Juanita Dugdale designed the cover and coordinated the graphic design and typography of the book. Deanna C. Medina helped collect and organize the illustrations and assisted with page layout and production. My associates and staff helped with information, plans, and other material. For the words, opinions, facts and "voice" of *Civil Architecture*, the responsibility is mine alone.

Index

About the Author

Richard Dattner heads his own architectural firm in New York City.
The firm has completed a wide variety of public projects, and has received
over 70 design awards and citations. Mr. Dattner was Adjunct Professor
of Architecture at The Cooper Union and the City College of New York,
and Distinguished Visiting Professor at the University of Wisconsin. A
Fellow of the American Institute of Architects, he has received the Medal
of Honor from the AIA New York Chapter and is the 1994 recipient of
the AIA's prestigious Thomas Jefferson Award for outstanding work in
public design.